Standing on a Reformed fo   ct
practical scaffolding to help   t-
ers to build lives of ongoing healing and sanctification. They recognize that
porn addiction isn't simply a lust problem or a stronghold that is corrected
quickly; rather than treat it as such, they take their readers on a patient
journey toward lasting wholeness.

—**Sam Black**, Vice President of Business Development, Covenant Eyes

Rescue Plan is an extremely practical resource, rooted in the gospel, for
porn strugglers and those who want to help them to find freedom. But
more than that, it unmasks the truth that these struggles can be common
problems for all God's people, at some time or another, in whatever stage
of life they find themselves. It offers real, concrete strategies for the power
of the gospel to break into strongholds of the heart in ways that lead to
inner transformation and change.

—**John Freeman**, Founder, Harvest USA; Author, *Hide or Seek: When
Men Get Real with God about Sex*

Ensnarement to the addiction of sexual sin can feel impossible to escape.
But no sin is too strong for Jesus to help you to overcome. Whether you
are fighting your own sin or helping someone else, *Rescue Plan* is packed
with practical, thoughtful truth, rooted in scriptural wisdom to help you
to lean on Jesus for help.

—**Garrett Kell**, Pastor, Del Ray Baptist Church, Alexandria, Virginia;
Author, *Pure in Heart: Sexual Sin and the Promises of God*

Pornography has morphed into a ubiquitous assault on human dignity
and the holiness of God. Jonathan and Deepak offer gospel wisdom to
engage this sin in a gracious yet pointed way. They provide specific, practical insights that will bring freedom from the clutches of pornography
through solutions that are drawn from God's Word. I recommend this book
to disciplers who are helping people in various stages of life to overcome
struggles with pornography.

—**Evan Marbury**, Licensed Therapist, Hope Counseling Services,
Chapel Hill, North Carolina; Pastor, Christ Central Church, Durham

I love three things about *Rescue Plan*. First, it's soaked in the gospel, which means it provides burden-lightening truth for its readers. Second, it delves into areas of pornography that the church has often shied away from. Third and finally, it offers not only practical wisdom but opportunity for deep reflection. Jonathan and Deepak have written a book for our age, and for the ages.

—**Ronnie Martin**, Lead Pastor, Substance Church, Ashland, Ohio;
　　Cohost, *The Art of Pastoring* podcast

The apostle Paul commanded us to "bear one another's burdens, and so fulfill the law of Christ." That is the heart of this book. Deepak Reju and Jonathan Holmes have provided a practical, biblical, and gospel-saturated guidebook to help Christians and the Christian church to bear the burdens of brothers and sisters in Christ who struggle with sexual sin. The book is remarkably candid, and the authors bring both years of pastoral experience and deep biblical conviction to this timely and urgent subject. We live in a world awash with pornography and its devastating consequences. Reju and Holmes offer sound and trustworthy care, saturated in gospel hope.

—**R. Albert Mohler Jr.**, President, The Southern Baptist Theological
　　Seminary

There has long been a gap in biblical counseling resources for women who are struggling with sexual sin. Typically, the church has assumed either that women don't struggle in this way or that women struggle in exactly the same way as men. Many thanks to Reju and Holmes for filling the gap with a comprehensive, hope-filled, and practical guide for sexual sinners regardless of gender, age, or life stage. This will be a much-used resource in my library.

—**Brenda Pauken**, Biblical Counselor, Sterling Park Baptist Church,
　　Sterling, Virginia

Porn grabs hold of a person, body and soul. Its grip is so cruel—so comprehensive—that folks tend to give up hope that freedom is even possible. Holmes and Reju take that experience seriously, even while offering confident guidance toward Jesus Christ, whose grip is much stronger than anything that threatens us.

—**Jeremy Pierre**, Professor of Biblical Counseling and Department Chair, The Southern Baptist Theological Seminary; Author, *The Dynamic Heart in Daily Life: Connecting Christ to Human Experience*

With a heart for both men and women who are ensnared by pornography, Deepak and Jonathan offer readers a compassionate understanding of how to break its addictive roots. Passing on what they have learned from helping strugglers in all life stages, they offer priceless practical tips, honest words of hope, and an invitation for strugglers to love Jesus more than their sin. I will be recommending this excellent resource often.

—**Darby A. Strickland**, Counselor, Christian Counseling & Educational Foundation; Author, *Is It Abuse? A Biblical Guide to Identifying Domestic Abuse and Helping Victims*

An indispensable resource! Deepak and Jonathan provide vital wisdom gained from the study of Scripture and through years of counseling to help us all to make war on the calamity of sexual sin. In this book you will find practical and critical steps to take in implementing a rescue plan. I am thrilled to see a new resource that equips us with biblical truth as we seek to strengthen our counsel. A practical, helpful, and applicable book, and an excellent resource! Read it. Apply it. Share it.

—**Shauna Van Dyke**, Executive Director, Association of Biblical Counselors; Founder and Executive Director, Truth Renewed Ministries

Rescue Plan is a timely resource for the person who wants to take seriously the Lord's Great Commission to make disciples and then teach them to observe everything Christ has commanded us. Sexual sin in the church might be one of the most dominant issues you'll face as you seek the Lord and as you seek to help others to pursue sanctification in Christ. This book is an important addition to what's already been written. It adds significantly to the conversation rather than just repackaging and repeating what is already out there. It is gospel saturated with Christ at its center but also helps disciplers understand how the gospel is intensely practical. Pastors, counselors, and anyone who is serious about the Great Commission, you need to read this book, and you need to have it in your library to reference in the future.

—**Greg Wetterlin**, Director, Restoration Ministries; Pastor of Men's Ministries, Faith Church, Lafayette, Indiana

In *Rescue Plan*, Reju and Holmes show the beauty, power, and sufficiency of Jesus to equip the body of Christ to care well for women and men who are dealing with sexual addiction. What a thoughtful work, filled with rich theology and practical wisdom. I can't recommend this book enough.

—**Jamaal Williams**, Lead Pastor, Sojourn Church Midtown, Louisville, Kentucky

RESCUE PLAN

RESCUE PLAN

CHARTING A COURSE TO
RESTORE
PRISONERS OF PORNOGRAPHY

DEEPAK REJU & JONATHAN D. HOLMES

P&R
PUBLISHING
P.O. BOX 817 • PHILLIPSBURG • NEW JERSEY 08865-0817

Unless otherwise indicated, Scripture quotations are from *ESV Bible* ® (*The Holy Bible, English Standard Version* ®). Copyright © 2001 by Crossway Bibles, a publishing ministry of Good News Publishers. Used by permission. All rights reserved.

Scripture quotations marked (NIV) are taken from THE HOLY BIBLE, NEW INTERNATIONAL VERSION®, NIV®. Copyright © 1973, 1978, 1984, 2011 by Biblica, Inc.® Used by permission. All rights reserved worldwide.

Scripture quotations from the New Testament use the ESV's alternate, footnoted translation of *adelphoi* ("brothers and sisters").

Italics within Scripture quotations indicate emphasis added.

In the counseling cases described throughout this book, names and identifying details have been changed to preserve anonymity.

Printed in the United States of America

Library of Congress Cataloging-in-Publication Data

Names: Reju, Deepak, 1969- author. | Holmes, Jonathan D., author.
Title: Rescue plan : charting a course to restore prisoners of pornography
 / Deepak Reju, Jonathan D. Holmes.
Description: Phillipsburg : P&R Publishing, [2021] | Includes
 bibliographical references. | Summary: "Drawing on the research and
 experience of two biblical counselors, this book provides concrete
 information and guidance on how to help pornography users in diverse
 circumstances to overcome addiction"-- Provided by publisher.
Identifiers: LCCN 2021027722 | ISBN 9781629953830 (paperback) | ISBN
 9781629953847 (epub)
Subjects: LCSH: Pornography--Religious aspects--Christianity. |
 Sex--Religious aspects--Christianity. | Pastoral counseling. | Peer
 counseling in the church. | Counseling--Religious aspects--Christianity.
Classification: LCC BV4597.6 .R4535 2021 | DDC 241/.667--dc23
LC record available at https://lccn.loc.gov/2021027722

To David Powlison,
who was a much beloved friend and mentor to both of us.

There are very few people who leave such an imprint on you that they rewrite your DNA and change the way you think and view life. David did that for us. Though we wrote this book, David's thoughts, words, love, and motivations sit on almost every page.

We still grieve his death but look forward to seeing him, hugging him, singing with him, and laughing together with him in glory.

Glory be to God.

CONTENTS

Introduction: How to Plan a Successful Rescue
Operation   9
A Note about *Rescue Skills*   17

PART 1: KNOW YOUR ENEMY

1. Sin Destroys Sex   21
2. The Prison of Addictions   31
3. An Addict's Four Foes   47

PART 2: KNOW THE LAY OF THE LAND

4. Masturbation Is Not What God Wants   65
5. Ten Strategies to Address Masturbation   79
6. The Similarities and Differences between Men and
   Women   99

PART 3: RESCUE THE PRISONER

7. Singleness: The Plight and Possibilities for Singles   125
8. Dating: When a Boyfriend or Girlfriend Confesses   149
9. Marriage: One Spouse Messes Up and the
   Other Feels Betrayed   169
10. Children and Teenagers: When Kids Get Caught
    and Parents Panic   193

Conclusion: Victory, Better Endings, and a Glorious
Savior   211

Acknowledgments   215
Appendix: A Godly Vantage Point on Sex   219
Notes   225
Resources for Fighting Pornography   239

INTRODUCTION:
HOW TO PLAN A SUCCESSFUL
RESCUE OPERATION

The year was 1941. The Japanese overtook the Philippines on December 8, just ten hours after their attack on Pearl Harbor. General John MacArthur fled to Australia in March of 1942, leaving 76,000 US soldiers to surrender to the enemy in April.[1]

The Japanese were cruel to American POWs. The prisoners were sent on the infamous Bataan Death March, an extended trek on which thousands of soldiers died due to starvation, lack of medical treatment, and their captors' unrestrained brutality. Trucks ran over soldiers who fell sick on the road, flattening and crushing them into the ground. Enemy soldiers forced POWs to sit in the sweltering heat without covering or had them pause within sight of cool water, killing any prisoner who attempted to break loose from the formation to get a drink.[2]

In December 14, 1944, one hundred fifty American troops were burned to death and executed by the Japanese at a POW camp at Palawan Island.[3] Fearful that the same fate awaited the five hundred US POWs at a camp in Cabanatuan, the US Army selected Colonel Henry Mucci, a natural leader who was adored by his men,[4] to lead the Army 6th Ranger Battalion to rescue them.

Colonel Mucci said, with characteristic passion in his voice, "It's going to be extremely dangerous. Some of you might not make it back."[5] But when the Army Rangers learned of the opportunity to rescue their fellow countrymen, not a single one turned down the opportunity.

Mucci's right-hand man was Robert Prince, a twenty-five-year-old Stanford graduate who had never seen combat up close. Mucci selected Prince to plan the entire operation. Mucci would get the troops to the edge of the prison at Cabanatuan, but Prince needed to piece together the rescue operation.

The key would be the element of surprise. Yet, as Prince planned, one thing struck him. The entire area around the prison camp was as flat as an Iowa or South Dakota plain and had no trees or structures.[6] How could the Rangers catch the enemy off guard if there was nothing to hide behind?

"I was very apprehensive," Prince later commented. "Any commander's greatest fear is the fear of failure. It preys on you. You have to keep your focus. You have to consider all the things that could go wrong, but then you have to quickly banish them from your mind. If you think about them too long, you can't go forward—you're paralyzed."[7]

Would Prince plan a successful rescue operation? Could he find a way to free the US POWs from their three years of misery?

THE RESCUE OF A BELIEVER'S SOUL

If you've picked up this book, it's probably because you are in the middle of your own rescue operation. It's not a special operations assignment in World War II, carried out against a brutal imperial army. Rather, your war is against the devil—and his weapons are anger, hatred, lies, selfishness, deceit, confusion, unbelief, and idolatry. Rather than enduring torture or starvation, the prisoner you seek to rescue is being harmed by the devil through pornography. You are helping a friend who looks at the forbidden—click, click, click. You've seen the pain and misery that porn brings him. Every time a struggler faces temptation, he feels as though a magnetic pull is dragging him back. He hates it but wants more. He feels ashamed and struggles to find God's forgiveness. His desires run amok. He gets further enslaved. Sadly, this becomes *the* preeminent battle of his life.

The battleground of a Christian's war is his heart. Like most wars, it is fought to be won or lost. There will be no peacekeeping treaty. God is jealous for his children's hearts, and he will not concede this territory to the devil (see Jer. 31:33; James 4:4–5).

Consider the apostle Peter's exhortation: "Beloved, I urge you as sojourners and exiles to abstain from the passions of the flesh, which wage war against your soul" (1 Peter 2:11). Peter asked the Christians of his day to refrain from the selfish passions of their sinful nature. Surrounded by the ungodly practices and customs of unbelievers, the Christians were to live as sojourners or exiles. They didn't belong, and so their lifestyle was supposed to look different from that of those around them. The same goes for every believer today—this world is not our home, and the practices of this world, such as the destructive habits of pornography use and masturbation, should be foreign to us as Christians. But, alas, they are not.

What is the purpose of a war? To destroy the enemy. As a discipler of a believer who struggles with pornography, you know this. You're helping a friend who is fighting to survive in her own personal war against porn. The selfish passions of her flesh are waging war— literally to destroy her soul. Scary, isn't it? The war raging inside her is between the Holy Spirit and her sinful flesh. She stares at a computer screen, with a tantalizing image staring back at her, and her flesh rages: "I want more." "Yes, this feels good." "Just a little bit longer." "Forget the truth, for a moment, and enjoy this." "God will forgive me." Click, click, click—she takes in more. But with each click, with each stare, with each selfish desire that is fed, the flesh wars against her soul and she sears her conscience with her sin. She has become a prisoner of the Enemy.

Depressing, isn't it? But there is hope. The fact that you picked up this book shows that the battle is not lost. You're still in the fight, and God stands alongside you, claiming the victory over the souls of his own children. Remember, the Scriptures say that God "yearns jealously over the spirit that he has made to dwell in us" (James 4:5).

God is jealous. He put his Spirit in believers, and he is eager to see their spirits worship him for all eternity.

Have you given up? If so, does it give you any hope to know that God "yearns jealously" for you and your struggling friend?

Welcome to the war for a believer's soul. This is your call to arms and a reminder that God stands alongside you, arm-to-arm, in the fight (see 2 Tim. 4:16–18). Sound the trumpet, and let's begin.

Pornography addiction is an addiction to sexual sin that overtakes a person's life. The person who has embraced pornography views naked people through images or videos. For their own selfish pleasure, men and women arouse themselves by viewing someone else's nakedness and (usually also) their sexual acts. Nakedness and sex are exposed, selfishly exploited, and consumed by a bystander who is not the husband or wife of the person or people involved.

The word *addiction* is a loaded term in our culture today. When we speak of addiction, we'll define this idea biblically. Think in terms of *voluntary slavery*—the struggler has chosen this sin so often that he's now enslaved to it. Or *desires run amok*—the struggler's carnal desires have become ruling desires that have overrun her life.[8]

In today's world, there are ever-expanding ways to engage sexual content and get addicted to it—sexting, engaging in phone sex, reading about sex in trashy fan fiction or erotic novels, viewing anime or virtual pornography, and so on. So, while we've written this book with an eye toward defeating pornography addictions, much of what we write applies to all kinds of troubling sexual sin.

HELPING THE HARD CASES OF PORNOGRAPHY

Who are you helping? Consider a sampling of stories.

Jayden was ashamed that he had fallen again. He'd started watching pornography in junior high and struggled on and off for years. It started with a click on an ad on a sports website so he could look at scantily clad women in the swimsuit issue of *Sports Illustrated*. The images awoke a toxic combination of curiosity and arousal that led him on a quest for more. His descent into the pit continued with photographs of naked women and then videos of men and women having sex. Chat rooms and phone sex quickly followed. He's fought his habit for years, but to no avail. It's been so bad for so long that he assumes things won't change. He'll battle sexual sin until he dies.

Pornography is talked about as a man's struggle. So the fact that Ellen looks at illicit pictures and videos is doubly shameful to her. She fights temptations and carnal desires alone. Shame plagues her like a rain cloud that follows her around. Her thoughts are no better: "There must be something wrong with me." "None of my other girlfriends talk about struggling with porn." Worst of all: "Maybe God has forgotten me."

Patrice thought the relationship was going really well. Dominic was thoughtful. They laughed together a lot. He led in spiritual conversations. Now, however, she is hurt and angry. After four months of dating, Dominic has confessed his porn addiction. He'd been battling it throughout their relationship and long before, but she had no idea. She really thought he was going to be the one. Now she isn't sure.

Peter was watching an illicit video when his wife walked in. He slammed his laptop shut and sat awkwardly as she stared at him. "Why did you do that?" "Do what?" "Shut the laptop like you have something to hide." At first he denied any wrongdoing. But Jenny was suspicious. She snooped around in the days that followed. It wasn't hard for her to uncover a mountain of evidence that he was watching porn with frightening regularity. She was crushed. She confronted him again, and he denied it. Now their marriage is in troubled waters with no rescue in sight.

Camille spends her days fantasizing about a man she knows at work. None of the guys at church ever pay attention to her. She hasn't been on a date in five years. Loneliness is painful. Erotic literature is her reading pleasure. Fantasies allow her to experience sex when it is impossible in the real world. She occasionally looks at pornography as well, though her conscience wrestles with it.

Ten-year-old Charlie saw porn for the first time after his parents gave him an iPad. They put the typical parental restrictions on, added Covenant Eyes, and falsely assumed those steps would keep him out of harm's way. They were dead wrong. Charlie is highly competent with technology. He found a workaround and started searching for porn. It didn't take long for him to find seductive pictures of naked women. Now, during his junior year of high school, he is looking two or three times a day, every day of the week. It is easy for him to rationalize his behavior: "I'll stop next time." "God will forgive me."

Every one of these scenarios is a mess of sin, guilt, lies, hiding, temptation, shame, self-justifications, hopelessness, foolish decisions, and hurt relationships. Change the names, circumstances, or even gender, and the underlying war remains the same—a battle to fight a sexual addiction that is ruining a believer's life.

What about you? You may be reading this book because your scenario resembles one of these. Or you may be a pastor, counselor, small-group leader, family member, roommate, close friend, or fellow church member who is looking to care for, counsel, and help a believer out of a pit. (From here on out, we'll use the term *helper* or *discipler* for any of these roles.) We've written this book primarily for the discipler, though we hope struggling Christians will benefit from it also.

A quick note on the use of pronouns: We understand that porn addiction is a problem for both men and women, so we alternate between masculine and feminine pronouns throughout this book. Much of the content applies to both men and women, regardless of the specific pronoun we have chosen for a given section.

What you need, and what we want to offer you, is a rescue plan—a way out of this mess. We're sending you twenty-seven miles behind enemy lines to retrieve prisoners of war. You're fighting against the world, the sinful flesh, and the devil (see Eph. 2:1–3). In this book, you will learn how to chart a course to rescue prisoners of pornography. It *is* possible to help an enslaved believer to find joy, freedom, and hope in Christ. This requires struggling believers to fight sexual sin, build healthy relationships, reengineer their views on sex, rework their desires, learn to better navigate temptations, grow in faith in Christ, and so much more. It's a tall order, but we can do it.

So come aboard, and buckle up.

WHAT LIES AHEAD

Here are the elements of a successful rescue operation.

In part 1, we get to *know our enemy*. Sin destroys sex. It attempts to ruin God's plan for our sexuality. Addictions imprison a believer and trap her. To help her, we've got to understand the nature of sexual addictions. And we'll think through the key ingredients to acting out in the moment: an addict's four foes of *access, anonymity, appetite,* and *atheism.*

In part 2, we get to *know the lay of the land.* This is important and practical background information about the terrain on which the war is fought. Masturbation is a common problem that is often paired with pornography. We've got to learn how to address masturbation to win this war. We've also got to understand similarities and differences between men and women. If we presume porn struggles are a man's problem and ignore the fact that many women are overrun with sexual sin, we've already set ourselves up for failure.

In part 3, we *rescue the prisoner*. It's time to put the information we've learned in parts 1 and 2 into action. Think of the difficult situations you encounter in daily life—a single man or woman who struggles with porn, masturbation, and fantasies; a dating couple in crisis after one party confesses his or her sexual sin; a spouse who is caught in addiction; and a teenager who has been hiding from his or her parents.

You'll find an application section at the end of each chapter called "Building a Rescue Plan." We'll offer personal reflection questions, potential problems, practical steps, and ways to pray. Slow down and make use of this section. Don't skip past it! You'll get more out of the book, and it'll strengthen your acuity and skills as a discipler.

Are you ready to begin? Let's get started with part 1, in which we'll get to know our enemy.

If you are a pastor, a counselor, or a ministry worker, you'll want to read *all* of part 3. You'll inevitably encounter each of these situations. Better to be prepared before they come knocking at your door. If you are helping someone in a specific situation, you should read parts 1 and 2, then jump to whichever chapter in part 3 most applies.

A NOTE ABOUT *RESCUE SKILLS*

This book is a companion to *Rescue Skills: Essential Counseling Skills for Restoring the Sexually Broken.*

Rescue Plan teaches you theory—explaining the nature of pornography addiction and what it looks like when it shows up in different stages of a person's life. *Rescue Skills* is about how to *interact* with a believer who struggles with pornography. Ideally, you will read both books, since *Rescue Skills* guides readers in developing more than twenty different practical skills, including

- listening with an active ear,
- targeting the heart,
- discerning fake repentance,
- recovering after a fall, and
- fighting battle weariness.

Rescue Plan is about *what, when,* and *why; Rescue Skills* is about *how.*

Picture this: You're talking with Harry, a Christian friend who confesses that he's struggled with pornography since he was twelve years old. He is now twenty-five. He's a member of your church and attends regularly. He's a part of a small group, but he's been vague about his addiction with the other men in the group. He stumbles late at night or on the weekends when he has much more time on his hands.

What do you do? What questions do you ask? Where do you take him in Scripture? How do you minister to his guilt and shame? What kind of accountability does he need? What heart issues motivate his acting out? What does he do after he falls? How can you help him to renew his relationship with the Lord? What do hope and help look like in this situation with this person?

Do you feel like you would know what to do in a conversation with Harry? If your answer is "I'm not sure" or "Definitely not," then we'd encourage you to read *Rescue Skills*.

PART 1

KNOW YOUR ENEMY

The Alamo Scouts were a group of behind-the-scenes intelligence gatherers. The two five-man squads were dispatched for a reconnaissance of the prison camp at Cabanatuan in advance of the Army Rangers' arrival. Led by Bill Nellist and Tom Rounsaville, the group initially failed at their task.

For two long days, they had done their best to survey the camp, but they still didn't have many details they needed. How many prisoners were in the camp? How many Japanese soldiers were guarding them? Were there tanks or any other heavy armored vehicles in the camp? If so, where were they stored? How many prisoners could walk, and how many were sick? Were there any ditches or ravines that could provide cover? Were there communication lines between the camp and the neighboring Cabanatuan City, and, if so, how many?

The famed Alamo Scouts were not living up to their reputation as an elite group. Why so little information?

"We can't get up close," Nellist explained to Colonel Mucci and Captain Prince. "It's flat as a pancake out there." The scouts had been unable to get near to the camp to gather the vital details needed to plan a successful rescue operation.

Mucci ripped off his sunglasses in frustration, revealing bloodshot eyes. "We've got to know more," he bellowed. "A *lot* more."

If they didn't gather the necessary information, the operation was bound to fail—and failure was not an option.[1]

You can't save a prisoner if you don't know what you're up against. To plan a successful rescue, you first need to *know your enemy*. That's what we'll cover in this first section.

1

SIN DESTROYS SEX

We Christians get embarrassed about our bodies. . . .
We are not sure whether bodies are good or bad;
it follows that we are not sure whether sex is good or bad.
—*Lauren F. Winner,* Real Sex

My sex life will be shaped and directed by whatever is my
street-level master. And I will only ever stay inside God's wise
boundaries when he is the functional ruler of my heart.
—*Paul David Tripp,* Sex and Money

Is the name Alan MacMasters familiar to you? Probably not, but I'm guessing you use something that he invented. In 1893, MacMasters invented the first ever electric bread toaster. Up until this point, if you wanted a nice warm piece of toast to slather butter and jam on, you'd need to hold it over an open flame or put it on some sort of metal grate.

Why are we talking about MacMasters and toasters? The reason is more important than you think. Let's say you're involved in a little home improvement project and you're in need of a hammer. When you ask your son to grab one for you, he hands you a toaster. You look at him incredulously and repeat, "I need a hammer! This is a toaster," to which your son replies, "Yeah, I know, but a toaster can still hammer the nail in." Can the toaster do this? Yes (probably with great damage to its shiny chrome exterior), but it wouldn't be in keeping with what the toaster was designed for.

What if you went ahead and used the toaster as a hammer? That would be to declare, "I know it was designed for toast . . . but I'm

21

going to use this toaster how I want to use it. If I want to use it to bang a nail into the wall and damage the chrome, I will!" How destructive it would be to use a toaster like a hammer. Alan MacMasters would want you to use a toaster to *toast bread*, not bang nails into a wall.

THE IMPACT OF SIN ON SEX

What's our point? We do the same thing when we use sex for selfish purposes and ignore God's intention for it. Every time a man or woman misuses sex, they make the very same declaration: "I know how God has designed sex . . . but I'm going use it how I want to use it. If I want to indulge in premarital sex or pornography and masturbation, then I will! I don't care about the damage it does to me and others." Sin prefers to misuse and mistreat what God has designed. Our sinful flesh, our oversexualized culture, and Satan all work together to misappropriate sex.

Today's culture writes its own script when it comes to sexuality. We live in an age in which each individual's sexual expression is considered his or her personal prerogative. We are told to do whatever makes us happy! Be whoever we want! Be free! Our surrounding culture tells us that this is especially true as it relates to sex and sexual identity. "You use your body however you want!" it says. "Sex is whatever you want it to be."

Embedded in this cultural narrative is a glaring fallacy. If sex is whatever you want it to be, then *ultimately sex is meaningless*. Journalist Alex Morris uncovered this fallacy in an interview he did with an artist, Curtis Roush, as part of a feature for *Rolling Stone*: "It's more fun to get [sex] out of the way and see how you connect, and then focus on who they are as a human. 'Are you interesting? Are you fun to be around? Great.' Sex isn't inherently a huge step. At the end of the day, it's a piece of body touching another piece of body—just as existentially meaningless as kissing."[1] If everyone defines sex however they want and to be whatever they want, then sex is certainly "meaningless." No surprise—defining sex however you want leads to using sex however you want. Sex quickly devolves into a dehumanizing and selfish venture.

If the devil convinces you that *ultimately sex is meaningless*, then he's won. The devil laughs as teenagers, singles, and spouses indulge in pornography and get addicted. He loves it when singles start hiding from their gospel communities because of shame. He relishes the degradation of trust in a marriage when a husband or wife looks at videos of sex. He wanders around the earth, looking for another Christian to consume, screaming things like, "Can't you see how many people I've messed up? Can't you see that I've won?"

Has the devil really won? Some days, as we come alongside struggling Christians in our oversexualized culture, it can certainly seem as though he has. As Christians, you and I need God to redeem sex (and our understanding of it) after sin has ruined it and Satan has messed it up. We need hammers for nails, not toasters as hammers. We need to help people to see God's purposes for sex, especially as we come to know it through faith in Christ.

That's the goal of this chapter—to see how sin destroys sex but how God redeems it. Most of our energy throughout this book will be spent on one specific iteration of sin's war: how the sins of pornography and masturbation ruin what God intends. But before we descend into the specific details of pornography struggles, we'll take this chapter to set out the redemptive storyline of our sexuality. And in hearing this story, we'll come to know God's vantage point on our sexuality. What does God want for us when it comes to sex?

SEX AS GOD INTENDED

Today we live in a technology-dominated, sex-driven culture that screams, "God doesn't matter" and "Sex matters more than anything else." Television and movies are laced with it or (at the very least) heavy sexual innuendo. The Internet is chock-full of pornographic content. You can't walk down the street or drive down a highway without seeing an advertisement that is sexual in nature. Biblical notions of sex, marriage, and sexuality have been abandoned, and adultery is common.[2] If we could examine people's hearts, we'd find that a consumeristic view of sex rules the day. In this view, the pursuit of sex is for *my* pleasure and for *my* fulfillment, and the person I'm having sex with is merely an object to be used for *my* selfish gain.

Given all the ways we see sex misused today, it can be easy for us to think that sex is inherently sinful. But Nancy Pearcey sums up the good news: "If we are ever tempted to think that sex is corrupt or dirty, we need to remind ourselves that it was God who created it in the first place."[3] Nothing in the opening pages of Scripture suggests that sex is dirty—rather, it is to be celebrated.

Sex is not sinful. It's God's good gift to us. As the sovereign Creator of humanity, God designed our bodies for good and godly purposes, which includes sex. This is why we have sexual organs and engendered differences. After God created the first man and woman, Adam and Eve, they were married and became "one flesh" (Gen. 2:24). The essential idea of "one flesh" is a physical uniting of the man and woman . . . what you and I call sexual intercourse. From the beginning, God intended for men and women to have sex in the context of a covenant relationship.

"God is the Creator of the human being, and simultaneously also the Inaugurator of sex and of sexual difference. This difference did not result from sin; it existed from the very beginning, it has its basis in creation, it is a revelation of God's will and sovereignty, and is therefore wise and holy and good. Therefore, no one may misconstrue or despise this sexual difference, either within one's own identity or in that of another person. It has been willed by God and grounded in nature." **—Herman Bavinck**[4]

Before the fall, sex was *pure, good,* and *safe*. Moses writes, "And the man and his wife were both naked and were not ashamed" (Gen. 2:25). Imagine that—a totally naked and transparent existence (they literally had no clothes on), with no awkwardness. God looked down on man and woman after he made them and declared them—sexuality and all—to be "very good."

SIN DESTROYS SEX

But Adam and Eve's perfect lives changed forever after Satan enticed them to break God's command. The moment they sinned, their eyes were opened, and they knew they were naked. At once, their nakedness—which previously had not been an issue—was now a liability. So what did they do? They sewed fig leaves together and made loincloths in order to cover themselves.[5] When they heard God coming, they "hid themselves from the presence of the LORD God among the trees of the garden" (Gen. 3:8). They couldn't stand to be in the presence of the Holy One anymore.

Adam and Eve went from guilt-free to guilty, from shameless to hiding, from naked to covered. Romans 5 tells us that their choice to disobey God brought sin to all mankind. Sexuality was never the same again. Because of the fall of humanity, our sexual desires became *self-centered* (we use people to satisfy our pleasure), *disordered* (we want what we should not have), and *idolatrous* (our desires become more important than God). In just the first few books of the Bible, we see the resulting spectrum of sexual sin:

- The men of Sodom's demand to have sex with Lot's two guests— and Lot's perverse offer of his daughters instead (see Gen. 19)
- The sexual assault of Dinah—Jacob and Leah's daughter (see Gen. 34)
- The prostitution of Tamar to Judah, her father-in-law (see Gen. 38)
- The attempted sexual assault and ongoing sexual harassment of Joseph by Potiphar's wife (see Gen. 39)
- The adultery of David and Bathsheba (see 2 Sam. 11)
- The incestuous rape of Tamar by her brother Amnon (see 2 Sam. 13)
- Solomon's engagement in polygamy (see 1 Kings 11)

Throughout Scripture, sexual sin is pervasive not in just the Old Testament but also the New. Many of the lists of sins in the Pauline

Epistles include warnings against sexual immorality (see Rom. 13:13; 2 Cor. 12:21; Gal. 5:19; Eph. 5:3; Col. 3:5). Sexual sin even became characteristic of some churches, like the church at Corinth (see 1 Cor. 5:1; 6:18; 7:1). Though online pornography did not exist in Bible times, the viewing and exploitation of another person's nakedness and sex for selfish gain did.

The scourge of sexual sin continues today. Pornography addictions expose the very same self-centered, disordered, and idolatrous tendencies. Sexual sin ruins our consciences and corrupts our minds. It brings shame, self-pity, self-loathing, disappointment, and confusion into relationships; it laces us with guilt; and it causes us to grow hopeless. It's a clear demonstration that sin destroys sex.

What can be done about this? As is often told, there came a great Rescuer, who would do more for these people than they could ever ask or imagine (see Eph. 3:20).

GOD'S RESCUE PLAN

In 1 Corinthians, the apostle Paul warns us about the penalty for sexual sin: "Do you not know that the unrighteous will not inherit the kingdom of God? Do not be deceived: neither *the sexually immoral*, nor idolaters, nor *adulterers*, nor men who practice *homosexuality*, nor thieves, nor the greedy, nor drunkards, nor revilers, nor swindlers will inherit the kingdom of God" (1 Cor. 6:9–10). This is not just bad news for the Corinthian church. It's a warning for all of us today who engage in sexual sin.

But Paul doesn't leave us there. He has good news for those who trust in Jesus: "You were *washed*, you were *sanctified*, you were *justified* in the name of the Lord Jesus Christ and by the Spirit of our God" (v. 11). Paul distinguishes between the unrighteous (who won't inherit the kingdom of God) and believers who trust in Christ. The sexually immoral, adulterers, and homosexuals are transformed— they are "washed," "sanctified," and "justified." They are made new in Christ. They are no longer what they once were. And we, as believers, should not go back to our old ways. (Paul says, "And such *were* some of you," in verse 11.)

Jesus rescued us when he died for the ungodly. Through his work on the cross, our sexual sins are redeemed. All that is dirty, unclean, and shameful has been atoned for and cleansed by God in Christ. We no longer fight to live outside God's parameters but find a fullness of humanity by doing what God asks of us—staying pure. As our affections for the Lord grow, our desires for what he wants rearrange what we want. Our pleasure no longer revolves around ourselves. What we want is not self-centered but others-centered. For example, in marriage, our attitude moves from "I want pleasure" to "How can I serve and satisfy my spouse?" The best marital sex is selfless, not selfish. What God intended in the garden of Eden—for us to be naked and not ashamed, to be pure and happy in God—is redeemed in Christ.

What a glorious truth for all who struggle with sexual sin, disordered desires, frustrations, and disappointments. Jesus is making everything new.

Jesus's work on earth offers us hope in another way as well. Jesus came and lived life like one of us . . . body and soul. He "became flesh and dwelt among us, and we have seen his glory . . . full of grace and truth" (John 1:14). Our Lord lived a perfect life—one that was free of sexual brokenness and immorality. How and why is this hopeful to us? Because Jesus shows it's possible to be holy in a physical body. Though we'll never be perfect like Christ, he demonstrates what greater holiness looks like. We strive to be more like Christ in this way.

Jesus was, as the author of Hebrews says, "in every respect . . . tempted as we are, yet without sin" (Heb. 4:15). He experienced sexual temptation, just like us, but he never gave in. In fact, he experienced the full force of temptation in a way that we who give in to it do not.[6] Jesus is sympathetic to our temptations since he also endured temptation. That gives us hope as we fight and await our full redemption. We have a Savior who really gets what we're going through, and we can take comfort in that fact.

When we see Jesus Christ, we see someone who suffered through temptation, even sexual temptation, in order that he might be a merciful and faithful Great High Priest for us (see Heb. 2:17–18).

27

Yet the extraordinary thing is that Christ never gave in and had sex. Todd Wilson explains, "No one was more fully human or sexually contented than Jesus, yet Jesus never engaged in a single sexual act. Think about it. Jesus never enjoyed the pleasures of sex, an erotic touch, or a lingering kiss. And he never indulged sexual fantasy or lust of the kind he roundly condemns."[7] Though God commends sex as a good gift for a committed married couple, Jesus shows what a sexually pure life looks like. He shows that purity is in fact possible.

Now the story comes full circle. God's good design—for sex to be a gift to married couples and for us to be pure in our singleness before we get married—is restored through Christ. Sin destroys sex, but Christ redeems sexual strugglers through the cross.

CONCLUSION: TOASTERS, SEXUALITY, AND JESUS

If Alan MacMasters had a clear purpose for toasters (to toast!), how much more must God have clear purposes for our sexuality. Although porn struggles can be wearisome, discouraging, and defeating, those struggles are not the end of the conversation. Sin does not have the last word. Christ does. Jesus is the rescuer of our souls. That's not just trite, hyper-spiritualized consolation—it's true.

Pause and think about that. Do you really believe that Christ will redeem the sexually broken? In an age in which sexual sin is an epidemic, it's hard to trust that Christ will clean up our sexual messes. But he can, and he will. What's required of you is faith in him (see 1 John 5:4–5). Both the goodness of sex and its corruption are important to understand as we roll out a plan to rescue strugglers.

BUILD A RESCUE PLAN

Personal Reflection

In what areas have you struggled with sexual sin? How does your view of sexuality compre and contrast with God's

28

view? Do you understand God's purposes for sex? Have you made sex into an idol or an ultimate thing or have you made it secondary? How can you trust in Christ to redeem your own views on your sexuality?

Potential Problems

It's common for believers who struggle with pornography to have a distorted view of sex. They are shaped more by the ungodly views of the world than by God's perspective on our sexuality. A part of our initial plan needs to be to revitalize and renew their view of sexuality.

Practical Step

Turn to the back of the book, to the appendix "A Godly Vantage Point on Sex" (page 219). Use this overview and its accompanying questions to start a conversation with the person you are discipling. Help him or her to contrast his or her view of sex with what God thinks about sex.

Prayer

Help me to be an instrument in your hands—one who helps my friend to renew and redeem his sexuality. Help me to believe that Christ can redeem anything. In Jesus's name, amen!

2

THE PRISON OF ADDICTIONS

Sexual sin brings desolation. It promises
excitement and pleasure, but delivers discontent and
insatiable craving. . . . It leads to an insane life.
—*David White,* Sexual Sanity for Men

A Christ-centered perspective on addictions should . . . be revolutionary.
—*Edward T. Welch,* Addictions: A Banquet in the Grave

What is happiness? "Happiness is the moment before you need more happiness," explained Jon Hamm's character, a serial adulterer and alcoholic on AMC's *Mad Men.*[1] Hamm reveals the ironic problem of addictions—they're a never-ending cycle of overpromising and underdelivering.

Want relief? You'll get it . . . for a few minutes. Then life comes back at you.

Want acceptance? You'll get it . . . but unfortunately the people on the other side of the screen are pure fiction.

Want an escape? You'll get it . . . but reality beckons with all its problems and burdens.

Want pleasure? Sure, it feels good . . . for a few minutes. Then you realize just how fleeting worldly pleasure is.

Get to know an addict, and you'll witness the dreadful after-maths of his attempts at wanton lust fulfillment. Guilt. Shame. Embarrassment. Anger. Self-hatred. Doubts. Promise making—his pull-himself-up-by-his-bootstraps assurance that *this* is the last time. He's done with it. He can't go on like this. Maybe he tells you about

31

his "slip-up" and hopes you'll give him silver-bullet advice to get him over the hump. Maybe he's been battling this addiction since he was a teenager. It's been a long and wearisome fight. Why is this so hard for him to kick? Why is this the one sin he just cannot put to death? Why can't he escape this prison?

If you're a helper, you know how bewildered you can feel when a struggler shares yet another fall. You think, "I don't get how or when she became addicted!" or "I don't know what else to say!" or "What else should I do to help him?" You may be tempted to shift from gospel hope to more behavioristic methods. Maybe it's time he gets a flip phone. Maybe she needs medication. Maybe he should go to bed earlier. If the struggler's addiction has become the perennial focus of your conversations, you may believe you have nothing left to offer.

Before you throw in the towel, we want to encourage you afresh to stay in the battle. Stay engaged. Hold on to this thought: your friend is *needy*, and you are *needed* in his life.

A starting point for helping a person who is enslaved to pornography is to understand addictions. That's the goal of this chapter—to offer a quick overview of addictions and how they work to imprison believers. A better understanding *of* the problem leads to better strategies for fighting *against* the problem.

"According to the Roman law, an *addictio* was a person who was enslaved through a judicial procedure. . . . When a debtor could not repay his or her debt, creditors could recover their losses using a legal procedure. . . . If proven that the debtor lack[ed] the means to repay, the praetor, or the justice, could turn the debtor into a slave. Today the term *addict* is used to denote a person who is bonded, enslaved, with a substance or any other activity that is pleasurable." —**Gil Simsic**[2]

CAN THE BIBLE HELP US TO UNDERSTAND ADDICTIVE HABITS?

The words *addiction* and *addict* never appear in Scripture. Yet if you open up the pages of the Bible, you'll see ideas that speak directly to the problem of addictions—the concepts of voluntary slavery, double-mindedness, foolishness, idolatry, and disordered desires. These five biblical facets capture the nature of addictions and refract a different aspect of this problem. God has a lot to say about addiction.

Voluntary Slavery

Together, the words *voluntary slavery* feel like a paradox. But bear with us for a moment. Addiction is *voluntary* because an individual makes choices to engage in destructive and sinful behaviors. As image bearers, each one of us is responsible for his or her choices. No person or thing makes a struggler engage in this behavior. Addiction can also be described as *slavery* because sin leads to bondage—the experience of destructive and sinful behaviors outside the control of an individual.

Hold the words *voluntary slavery* in tension, and you see the basic building blocks of any addiction. It starts with a temptation and a dumb conscious choice.[3] The body gets a jolt of satisfaction, and a desire is awakened. But with each foolish decision, the impulses of the mind, the cravings of the heart, and the arousal of the body get more entangled, desires grow out of proportion, and a Christian becomes enslaved. Addiction moves from one foolish choice, to a carnal pursuit of sin many times, to slavery, and, finally, to death. The first time a man or woman looks at pornography, he or she is titillated but not addicted. The sight is powerful but not enslaving. Yet if he or she keeps coming back, after a few months the sin will progress to a place where the fool is in bondage.[4] (We'll look at this process more closely in the second half of the chapter.)

Nevertheless, in this dreadful combination—voluntary slavery— we also find hope. Because addiction is enslaving, the addict must acknowledge that he is not in control and must surrender to God. The Lord alone can change the struggler's will and free him by the power of his gospel. At the same time, because addiction is voluntary, the struggler must personally fight against it. To just "let go and let God" is not effective.

One Voluntary Choice

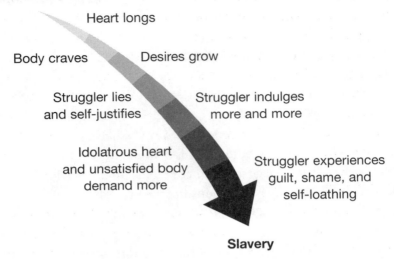

Fig. 2.1. The Descent into Slavery

Paul holds out the tension of *work* and *surrender* in Philippians 2:12–13 when he writes, "Work out your own salvation with fear and trembling, for it is God who works in you, both to will and to work for his good pleasure." The addict needs to work it out. Take responsibility. Do something about it, lest his selfishness festers. But he also must recognize that God works in him to change him for good—there is no room for a self-righteous attitude that says to God, "I can do this on my own. I don't need you."[5]

Voluntary slavery. Work and surrender. Holding these things in dynamic tension adds depth to our understanding of addiction.

Double-Mindedness

Sin makes us double-minded. The apostle Paul writes, "I do not understand my own actions. For I do not do what I want, but I do the very thing I hate. . . . For I have the desire to do what is right, but not the ability to carry it out" (Rom. 7:15, 18). Because of the "sin that dwells within [him]" (vv. 17, 20), Paul continues to do the very thing he hates. He has desires to do what is right, but he does not do what he wants. He's double-minded.

34

We're *all* double-minded, every one of us, but double-minded-ness is especially pronounced in those with addictions. The sexual struggler both hates her sin and loves it. She hates it the moment after her guilt and shame kick in. However, give it time, and her cravings resurface, her heart longs again, and her body wants more. Her affections for the addiction show themselves again. She becomes trapped by her conflicting desires. The addict's love for her sin returns with a vengeance. Yet she wants it to be gone and her love for Christ to be greater.

Foolishness

If you read through Proverbs and look closely at the proverbial fool, you'll notice that he looks strikingly similar to an addict. The epitome of addiction is spurning wisdom, insight, and a godly life (see Prov. 1:7). An addict is not open to correction (see 12:1); rather, he is convinced in his own mind that he is right (see 12:15). If you try to speak to him, he despises the good sense in your words (see 23:9). He lacks sense (see 8:5) and trusts in his own mind (see 28:26). We have sat with alcohol, drug, and porn addicts, pleading with them to flee their sinful lifestyles, only to hear them respond, "I don't need help" or "Leave me alone" or "I can handle it." Can you see the self-righteousness and pride of a fool in all this?

It doesn't stop there. There's more. Proverbs reveals that the addict takes no pleasure in understanding (see 18:2). His speech is crooked (see 19:1) and hasty (see 29:20), and he is prone to quarreling (see 20:3). His mouth is his ruin as it pours forth folly (see 15:2; 18:7). In fact, he flaunts his folly (see 13:16). If given a chance, he will wound loved ones and friends (see 26:10). Addicts typically have a string of broken relationships because of their reckless behavior and attitudes.

An addict's cravings and desires overrun his life. The book of Proverbs teaches that he will not turn from his evil desires (see 13:19). He returns to his foolishness and often repeats it, like a dog returning to its vomit (see 26:11).

Idolatry

An idol is not just a wooden or metal statue of a false god that a person bows down to and worships.[6] It's anything you put ahead of the Lord. Whatever you revere and love more than God, you've turned into an idol. What's behind this? An "exchange" that Paul talks about in Romans 1. We give up truth for a lie and worship creation rather than the great Creator (see v. 25).

You don't stick a wooden or metal idol on your dashboard as you drive to work. Idolatry goes much deeper—down to the desires of your heart. Your desires for power, adventure, affirmation, control, pleasure, recognition, significance, and happiness motivate your idolatry. The idol—whatever it is—is just a means to achieve these desires.[7]

Mark lusted after bodies on a screen, but he told us that what got to him was the way the women looked at him. His wife picked at and demeaned Mark, but these naked women looked longingly at him. It was as if they were saying with their eyes, "I want you." Mark's sense of being desired felt so good, especially after days of conflict with his wife. He used pornography to get the affirmation that was absent in his marriage.

Ruth longed for control in her life. She cheated and stole to get her addictive fix of porn and sexual sin. She manipulated men to sleep with her. She lied to her accountability partner so she didn't have to give up her sin.

With idolatry, the ultimate question is who will you worship? What's your ultimate allegiance (see 1 Kings 18:21)? Mark and Ruth had given themselves over to their idols. In their idolatry, they turned their backs on God and not only chose his creation over him but ultimately chose to walk into the self-made prison of addiction and throw away the key. *Self*-satisfaction, *self*-favoring, *self*ishness, and *self*-glory. These are the desires that rule an addict's heart and life. Sexual sin led Mark and Ruth away from God and put them into a penitentiary.

Disordered Desires

Our *hearts* have passions, desires, and cravings (see James 1:14–15; 4:1). The heart of the addict wants something—pleasure, recognition, comfort, or happiness. It covets and is greedy to satisfy its desires. If an addict's heart stands as the command center of her soul, the desires of her heart drive what she does.[8] If she wants affirmation, she'll spend time with those who give it to her. If she wants to get rid of her Saturday afternoon boredom, she'll access pornography.

Our *bodies* also have cravings (see Phil. 3:19). Sexual sin involves arousal, lust for physical satisfaction, and physical relief for pent-up tension. A porn struggler merely needs to recall a naked image and turn it over in his mind to feel a physical reaction as his body is stirred from its slumber.

Sexual sin combines the cravings of our bodies and hearts in a powerful one-two punch. We are drawn not just to what our hearts want but to what our bodies crave.

There are good and right desires for these things, such as a man or woman's desire for marriage (see Prov. 18:22) or a husband or wife's hope for intimacy with his or her spouse (see the entire Song of Solomon). But there are also selfish, disordered desires, such as the longing for pornography and masturbation. Much of your work involves cultivating the right desires and starving the wrong desires (see Rom. 13:14; 1 Peter 2:11). An important part of godliness is the discipline of our bodies ("I discipline my body and keep it under control"—1 Cor. 9:27). Freeing an addict involves helping him not just to reorder the desires of his heart but also to discipline his body.

THE CYCLE OF PORN ADDICTION

Each person you meet and disciple is unique. Yet there are patterns that ring true in nearly every story of addiction to pornography: the persistent stubbornness of sin, the cries of regret and accompanying shame, the heartache over broken promises, the resolve to finally be done with it only to fall into it again. Something about the relentless stubbornness of these patterns of sin seems to drain the life out of an addicted believer.

As we've counseled person after person, we've learned that every addiction has a typical cycle. How does Scripture speak, and speak vividly, to this spiral of addiction? The apostle James gives us an incisive look into the inner workings of sin. Read his description:

> Let no one say when he is tempted, "I am being tempted by God," for God cannot be tempted with evil, and he himself tempts no one. But each person is tempted when he is lured and enticed by his own desire. Then desire when it has conceived gives birth to sin, and sin when it is fully grown brings forth death. (James 1:13–15)

Let's take this passage slowly and parse out James's description of a person's spiral into sin: he or she is tempted, lured, and enticed into full-blown sin, which brings death.

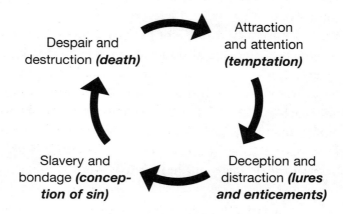

Fig. 2.2. The Cycle of Addiction

"By [God's] design, tests provide the opportunity to endure in faith, to grow strong, and to receive a crown. Yet God knows and controls all things. He knows that some will face tests and fail. So the same event is a test from one perspective, for one person, and a temptation from another perspective, for another person." —**Daniel Doriani**[10]

38

Attraction and Attention (Temptation)

We start with an initial temptation. As James shows us, a person is fully responsible for how he acts in the moment of temptation. If he chooses to rely on the promises of the Lord, then his temptation becomes an opportunity for him to have his faith strengthened and matured.[9] If he chooses to run down the path laid out in James 1, his temptation becomes an opportunity for sin.

We live in a world of temptations that scream out, "Pay attention! Wake up. Don't you want me?" Their initial attractions quickly and subtly lead us to dedicate our attention to them. This dynamic plays out more often than we acknowledge. Think of a middle-aged woman who is checking out at her local store when a photograph of a shirtless man on a magazine captures her eye. Combined with the titillating byline, it's enough for her to steal a furtive second glance. It's caught her attention.

Listen to how a struggler describes the journey from stolen attention to sexual sin:

> The luring temptation of pornography starts with an itch. The itch could come from a memory, from a passing jogger, from an innuendo, from a sense of inadequacy, or from myriad more sources. The itch is always subtle. It starts with noticing something enticing. Noticing becomes wondering, and wondering turns to scheming, and scheming leads to satisfying the lust. There is a sense that once you've entered into this lust cycle, there is no escaping it until it is satisfied. It is a ravenous wolf.

What a person pays attention to can send her down a self-destructive path. So start by considering what or who is grabbing your friend's attention.

Deception and Distraction (Lures and Enticements)

Now that the person is paying attention, we move into the next stage of the addiction cycle. The bait lures and entices. James employs the imagery of fishing or hunting—a hunter luring his prey out into the open or a fisherman dropping a lure in the water in hopes of catching a fish for his evening meal. The lure dangles in the water, capturing the glinting light of the sun. Seeing it, the fish moves just a little closer to its grave.

"'Desire' is like the hook with its bait, that first entices its prey and then drags it away. If the superficial attractiveness of 'desire' is not strenuously resisted, a person can become 'hooked' on it, unable to escape from its all-powerful lure." —**Douglas Moo**[12]

Unlike a fish, an addict can't blame the bait and the hook for snaring her. James tells us that the problem lies with the greedy desire in her heart. That desire "lures" and "entices" the sinner. Don't blame the titillating picture on *Cosmopolitan* or the scantily dressed man or woman on the street. Blame the war of desires in a sinner's heart. Carnal desires lure, then hook, this person and drag him or her down the path toward death.[11]

Hunters and fishermen rely on camouflage to capture their prey. It should be no surprise that their approach is cloaked in deception and distraction. Likewise, it would be odd if an appeal to sin came out in the open: "Come, indulge your lusts, and forget the God who loves you." No, camouflaged desires take a bit of the truth but distort it enough to get believers to take the bait.

- "I've had a hard day at work, and a little glance and enjoyment never hurt anyone."
- "Things have been rough at home lately, and I deserve a break right now."
- "It's not like I'm going to sleep with her."
- "Reading this trashy novel is different from looking at pornography."

What do you hear? A little bargaining and a whole lot of

self-deception. Something good (relief, happiness, joy) gets twisted and distorted into something that will become an addict's downfall rather than his good. Initial luring and enticement turn into seduction.

Slavery and Bondage (Conception of Sin)

The trap has been set, the prey has moved forward, and the trap has been sprung. Unfortunately, more often than not, the prey doesn't know she's been caught! The cycle of addiction starts with one voluntary choice. But if a believer gives herself—cognitively, emotionally, and behaviorally—over to what has ensnared her, James tells us that she'll descend into a pit of slavery. Seducing desires give birth to sin.

Herein lies the power of an addiction. It demands more and more from a person while delivering less and less. *Overpromise and underdeliver* is the marketing byline of addiction. And yet addicts continue to believe that at any point they can get themselves out of the trap. They are spiritually blind to their perilous position.

The words of John Bunyan ring true here:

Sin, rather than 'twill out of action be,
Will pray to stay, though but a while with thee;
One night, one hour, one moment, will it cry,
Embrace me in thy bosom, else I die:
Time to repent [saith it] I will allow,
And help, if to repent thou know'st not how.
    But if you give it entrance at the door,
    It will come in, and may go out no more.[13]

Sin demands more and more of a believer's worship, promising her ultimate fulfillment and satisfaction—then time and time again begging, "Just once more." Here's how another struggling believer describes it:

My sin had mastered me. I was a slave. I would indulge in porn at work for hours, and I was missing deadlines and not focused on my work. I would stay up all night, indulging my flesh, looking for just the right picture or video to gratify myself with. When I was finished, I would repeat this routine three or four times in one night. There were times when I got only two hours of sleep because I had stayed up all night looking at porn. I was out of control, and I could no longer choose anything else because it had control of my heart. Oh, there were times when I would go a week or more without looking at it, but as soon as the craving returned, I would fall again without any resistance. I loved my sin, but it was controlling me and ruining my life.

All the lies that pornography peddles come into full view here. The matrix of voluntary slavery, foolishness, and idolatry is on full display. Repeated personal indulgence of sin and self-gratification led to this struggler's inevitable downfall and sin's total control over his life.

Despair and Destruction (Death)

Irony comes full circle in James's illustration. The birth process that promises life delivers the exact opposite: death. The fish, swimming blissfully upstream, unaware of its surroundings and environment, sees what appears to be lunch. Next thing you know, the fish *is* lunch.

John Freeman describes it well: "No one sets out to get addicted to sin. Rather, we get hooked on, addicted to, and oriented toward the things to which we give our hearts on an ongoing basis. We start to become like the things we go to for life, and over time our life becomes chaotic and disordered, and we find ourselves as powerless and dead as the idols we look to."[14] Time and time again, we have heard stories of how this process plays out. We've heard the cries, despair, and disbelief of husbands who have thrown away their marriages for a night of pleasure. We've sat with singles who have ruined relationships or lost jobs because their addictions took over their lives. We've heard the proclamations and declarations of "I don't know why I keep doing this!" You can see an addiction's utter destruction up close as you glance at those who have been overrun by their carnal desires.

What's the Point of Studying the Addiction Cycle?

Why go into so much detail about the inward pathology of sin? If we want to understand the mind and heart of a pornography struggler, we have to know their inner workings. If we have "embedded in our minds the subtle way in which temptation moves from stage to stage until inexorably it comes to death and hopelessness, and despair," Sinclair Ferguson writes, we can "recognize it in its first risings" and be aware of its final destination.[15] We need to understand that repeatedly entertaining and engaging sinful desires will lead to negative spiritual, relational, physiological, and emotional results.

THE KEY TO THE PRISON

How do the sexually addicted or enslaved find true freedom? By grinning and bearing it? Going to Sexaholics Anonymous meetings? Getting therapy? Changing up their habits? If these methods sound less than promising, it's because they are. Even non-Christians acknowledge the futility of addressing addiction through self-help mechanisms: "It's almost impossible to overcome an addiction by sheer force of will."[16] No, we must look in a different direction. What if the solution to sexual sin isn't exclusively to say no to one thing but to say yes to a better thing? To actually believe that there is something better for us to give our affections, trust, and loyalty to?

John Bunyan's classic work, *The Pilgrim's Progress*, tells of an unfortunate detour that Christian and Hopeful take on their way to the Celestial City. While traveling, the pilgrims end up imprisoned by the Giant Despair after wandering into his land. Each passing day grows worse and worse, until Christian begins to believe that perhaps the only way out of his situation is to die.

But then Christian awakens with a newfound perspective: "What a fool am I thus to lie in a stinking dungeon, when I may as well walk at liberty! I have a key in my bosom, called Promise." He takes the key out of his pocket, opens the prison door, and releases himself and his friend from the prison! Door after door that had barred their escape opens with ease as Christian uses his key of Promise to pass each barrier. Bunyan records their escape: "They went on, and came to the King's Highway, and so were safe."[17]

How often is an enslaved addict like Christian and Hopeful, stuck and imprisoned in a dungeon seemingly without hope of freedom?

Where does the addict find hope? The key—yes, the key—is what it has always been: the good news of our freedom in Christ Jesus. It is the very words he speaks to his disciples and to us today: "The thief comes only to steal and kill and destroy. I came that they may have life and have it abundantly" (John 10:10).

Friend, these are the words of life that we must share with those who feel hopelessly enslaved to their sin. It is not enough for them to merely understand the sinfulness of their sin. They must embrace the abundant life that Jesus came to earth, lived, died, and rose again for them to have in him! These promises are foundational to the rescue plan that we'll put together throughout this book.

BUILD A RESCUE PLAN

Personal Reflection

Consider your perspective on addictions. Have you grown in your understanding of addictions? Do you think biblically about addictions? Do you know where to go in the Bible to learn more about addictions? If not, who can teach you more?

Potential Problems

Sadly, believers can be much more influenced by a hopeless and ungodly perspective on addictions and addictive cycles than by a distinctly biblical perspective.

Practical Step

First, take the five biblical categories—voluntary slavery, double-mindedness, foolishness, idolatry, and disordered desires—and talk through each idea with your friend. Apply each concept to the specifics of her situation. Second, trace out the ways she has been trapped in the addictive cycle.

Prayer

Lord, help me to think with a biblical lens. I want to know your Word and use it wisely in the life of my friend. Help me to model my trust in the Word and in the marvelous Savior who reveals himself through the Scriptures. In Jesus's name, amen!

3

AN ADDICT'S FOUR FOES

*Our problem is that we walk in unbelief. We fail to believe
that God cares or that he desires to enter into our struggles with
the sins of lust, pornography, and sexual temptation.*
—*John Freeman,* Hide or Seek

*Those entrenched in porn tend to live suffocatingly small lives,
constantly looking for their next fix. Those who begin to find
freedom begin inhabiting a larger, more colorful existence.*
—*Matt Fradd,* The Porn Myth

Manuel is sitting in his room, all alone, at 10:32 p.m. The door is
shut, and his phone and laptop are on his desk directly across from
him. He could go to bed, but he's feeling the pressure of fierce temptations. He feels aroused. His thoughts have been on an attractive
woman he saw at the gym this afternoon. There is a war raging in his
heart, and he wants to make a godly choice. His flesh pitches him
lies, all of which attempt to justify his sin: "Just one more time, and
then you'll stop." "You deserve it."

What will lead Manuel to act out? Four ingredients enable a
fall—*access, anonymity, appetite,* and *atheism.*[1] Remove any one of
these four *A*s, and you make acting out much less likely.

In our effort to rescue prisoners of pornography, we're getting to
know the enemy. These four *A*s are formidable foes. The goal of this
chapter is to understand them and figure out how to disrupt them
so their power is broken. What does a discipler need to know to help
his struggling friend?

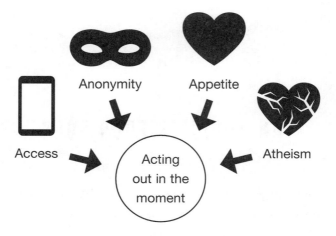

Fig. 3.1. The Four *A*s

ACCESS

In the age of the Internet, access to an online world is available virtually everywhere. That creates a *huge* problem for porn addicts because the Internet is littered with sexually explicit material of every description. Thus, open access is dangerous for any struggler's soul. Though the Internet can be used for great good, it also causes extraordinary harm.

A common strategy for fighting porn addiction is to restrict strugglers' access. We take away their freedom in order to protect them from themselves. Their pride makes them think, "I can handle this," but they are wrong. Until they grow in maturity in Christ, the desires of their flesh are too strong, and their self-control is too weak.

You Need to Be Radical

Our approach to limiting access is shaped by Jesus's words in Matthew 5:

You have heard that it was said, "You shall not commit adultery." But I say to you that everyone who looks at a woman with lustful intent has already committed adultery with her in his heart. If your right eye causes you to sin, tear it out and throw it away. For it is better that you lose one of your members than that your whole body be thrown into hell. And if your right hand causes you to sin, cut it off and throw it away. For it is better that you lose one of your members than that your whole body go into hell. (vv. 27–30)

He reminds us of the seventh commandment: do not commit adultery. But he takes the command one step further. He's not just talking about the physical act of adultery. Christ expands the definition—if a person looks at another with lustful intent in his heart, it is as if he too has committed adultery. An addict doesn't need to touch a woman to commit sin. He merely needs to look at her lustfully—and he does that every time he looks at porn.

Jesus goes on: "If your right eye causes you to sin, tear it out and throw it away. . . . If your right hand causes you to sin, cut it off and throw it away" (Matt. 5:29–30). He's using exaggeration for effect. The point is not that a sinner should actually do physical harm to herself but that she should understand how serious sexual sin is. Christ uses graphic imagery to say, "Be radical. Don't take a soft approach to fighting sexual sin. Brutally cut it out of your life."

Pause and think for a moment. As a discipler, start with your own approach to sin. Are you radical in cutting it out of your life? Think about your last bout with sin—what did you do? If you are not ruthless with your own sin, how do you expect others to follow suit?

On their own, addicts typically aren't radical in cutting off their sin. That's the case with Preston. He looks at porn because he's held on to access points, and he's grown too comfortable with his sin to cut it out. Rationalizations, excuses, and a love for his sin encourage him to hold on. Preston often thinks, "This will be the last time," or he lets himself off the hook by saying, "Everyone's doing it, not just me." He yearns for the naked photos and spends a lot of his time scheming how and when to look at them again.

Christ said to *be radical*. When you talk to an addict, do you plead and exhort him to take a more radical approach? We often say to strugglers, "Be brutal in cutting off access points." Get the person you are discipling to measure her last few months against Jesus's words. Has she taken drastic measures, or has she made excuses, delayed making adjustments, or continued to hide? Has she tolerated her sin, coddled it, maybe even welcomed it, and, in so doing, continued to give it a chance to ruin her life?

Many porn strugglers don't like losing access to the Internet, and so they fight against restrictions. You've heard the complaints: "How do I live without the Internet? I need it to do my job. . . . I've got to check my email. . . . I need it to connect with my friends. . . . I must have it for X, Y, and Z." Our response? There are consequences for sexual sin. The person should have thought about these consequences before he or she acted out. What is better—for your friend to lose an eye or hand but walk toward heaven or for her to run toward hell? If she chooses to indulge her sin, to ignore God's commands, to disobey and shake her fist at God, then her *rebellion* and *foolishness* will lead to death.[2] If she wants to grow in holiness, it will require sacrifice.

Fighting sin is serious business. Don't let your friend indulge her sin. What drastic steps can she take today to cut off her access to pornography? If she confesses looking at porn the previous week, your conversation should revolve around her access point and how to cut it out. Show zero tolerance for her sexual sin. Graciously and lovingly exhort your friend to get rid of access points!

Strategies for Closing Off Access Points

Here are some practical steps to consider as you help an addict to get rid of his access points.

1. Ask the porn addict about *every* e-device he owns.
2. Encourage him to get a software monitoring program, such as Covenant Eyes, and to put it on all his devices.
3. Get rid of standard web browsers and rely on a browser that is carefully monitored.
4. Get rid of the applications store. If he needs to download a new app onto a tablet or phone, provide him with access only temporarily.

5. Use special restrictions to cut out the web browser and app store, set time limits, and so on. Make sure the restrictions code is known only to an accountability partner. If the addict knows it, he will remove the restrictions in a moment of weakness and act out.
6. Get rid of all apps that have an embedded browser.

What's the principle behind these six points? We're removing control from the addict and giving it to others because the addict can't steward the freedom of open access.

The *nuclear option* is to get rid of televisions, tablets, phones, and laptops for a period of time. In our Internet age, that's hard to do, but it is viable, especially if the Internet is available in safe settings, such as a workplace that monitors its own computers.

There are so many backdoor ways to get Internet access or pornographic content. For instance, you can use online GIF generators to get pornographic GIFs. You can view pornography without ever leaving Twitter or access a web browser using a map application. And the list goes on. The flesh is very creative!

If an addict does need access for some legitimate reason, such as to download an application for work, then the addict should notify his accountability when an access point is opened and follow up when the access point is closed. If the accountability doesn't hear back soon, he should get in touch with the addict directly. Maturity is demonstrated when the addict takes initiative on these matters and is open and honest about what's going on.

ANONYMITY

Because of his guilt and shame, a struggler typically hides his pornography use. He may sit in a bedroom by himself or in an office with the door closed. If he is around others, he may orient his screen so that no one can see what he is doing. It's rare for strugglers to view porn in coffee shops or in the middle of open areas where people are going back and forth. Rather, they pursue isolation and anonymity.

Many women do feel comfortable reading erotic fiction in the open, now that it is more accepted in the mainstream. I (Jonathan) remember being at the community pool a few years ago and counting five women reading *Fifty Shades of Grey*. You can read more about this in chapter 6, where we discuss women, porn struggles, and erotica.

Solomon writes, "Whoever isolates himself seeks his own desire; he breaks out against all sound judgment" (Prov. 18:1). The one who deliberately isolates himself is focused on his own desires. As he feeds his sexual urges, his selfishness grows, and his corrupt desires become the centerpiece of his life. His selfishness separates him from community and, even worse, makes him unfriendly to those who should matter the most.

Pornography pulls an addict away from the very thing he or she needs—*God's wisdom available through God's people*. The one who isolates himself because of his desires "breaks out" against wisdom. The sound judgment that leads him down safe paths is abandoned or, even worse, mocked. He ignores or discards the wisdom that is available from a few choice godly friends or in his local church community. In this way, isolation can kill a person's soul.

Isolation allows addicts like Manuel and Preston to keep a safe distance from accountability relationships and community. And, in some cases, a consequence of isolation is that the addict remains unknown to others. We can't press into Manuel and Preston's lives if they hide, avoid accountability, put up protective walls, and refuse to be vulnerable about their sin struggles.

Why does a struggler act in this way? Sin likes to hide, and sexual sin in particular has a field day when it is kept secretive and hidden. It prefers darkness, which, in the Bible, is associated with an immoral, sinful life apart from God. The apostle John warns us, "If we claim to have fellowship with him [God] and yet walk in the darkness, we lie and do not live out the truth" (1 John 1:6 NIV). We are hypocrites if we claim to love God and, at the same time, coddle sexual sin.

One of the antidotes to sexual sin is to yank it into the light. God is light, and in him there is no darkness at all (see 1 John 1:5). As a struggler steps into his light, he repents (see Mark 1:15), confesses (see Prov. 28:13; 1 John 1:9), and exposes his sexual sin (see Eph. 5:11–14).

Strategize to get rid of anonymity in an addict's life. For example, an addict will watch pornography and masturbate late at night, alone in a room, with the door closed. That's what Preston does. He isolates himself so that he can sin. Lily, a graduate student, studies for long days and nights at home by herself, where no one will know if she chooses to view porn.

- If Preston and Lily are not talking to anyone about their sin, the first step is for them to open up and get others involved in their lives. They need to take a step out of darkness and toward godly relationships.
- Since Preston struggles late at night, we ask him to give his laptop to his roommate at 9 p.m., to hang out in more trafficked parts of his living situation, such as the living room, and not to shut his door until he's ready to go to sleep.
- We also ask Preston to always keep his office door open. When he's overwhelmed, he's not allowed to shut the door and plunge into porn. He should turn his desk so the screen is visible to employees who walk by his office.
- We ask Lily to study in public places, such as the local library or coffee shop. Long periods of study alone at home often lead her to act out.
- We encourage Lily to tell her friends to hold her accountable to not be home alone for extended periods of time.

APPETITE

Men and women have passions, desires, and motivations that drive what they think and do (see Gal. 5:16–17). We all have cravings or *appetites*. Sex. Coffee. Good food. Fun. Comfort. Power. Success. You name it, someone wants it. But imagine a desire that takes over a person's life and becomes a *ruling* desire. That's what your addicted friend is fighting—a desire that he or she has fed, nursed, and cultivated until it's grown big and strong. We saw this in detail in the last chapter.

You could think of this desire as a dragon: a tall, ugly, scaly, fire-breathing, beady-eyed beast generated by a struggler's sinful nature. Whenever a struggler looks at pornography, he throws the beast a thick, juicy steak. He is making provisions for the sinful nature, satisfying its desires (see Rom. 13:14). The more he feeds it, the more it grows, and grows, and grows. It always wants more. It's never satisfied. Eventually, it takes over.

To fight the dragon is to ally with the Holy Spirit in the war with the sin nature. The apostle Paul proclaims, "The desires of the flesh are against the Spirit, and the desires of the Spirit are against the flesh, for these are opposed to each other, to keep you from doing the things you want to do" (Gal. 5:17). The dragon's power is destroyed when the struggler starves her sinful nature's desires and puts them to death. Some days, those desires get the best of a struggler, and the dragon wins as she gives in to temptation.

Adelynn felt that way most days. She'd been losing her battle with a porn addiction for over a year. There were dozens of moments every week in which she felt as though her selfish cravings for porn had overtaken her life. Other days, she found victory as she walked in the power of the Spirit who dwelled in her. A year later, with a lot of help, prayer, adjustments to her life, and brutal honesty with God and friends, she saw tangible changes in her addiction.

Although we teach addicts how to handle temptation and how to restrict access, it's the desires that rage *within them* that are the ultimate problem. As a discipler, are you focused only on fighting off temptations, or are you also working to curb the struggler's corrupt desires? Are you paying attention to the war within? Practically speaking, you can't focus only on eliminating access and anonymity. You should talk to an addict not just about his external circumstances but also about his appetites. Ask him,

- What do you love and hate right now?
- How is selfishness or pride ruling your heart?
- What do your actions show you that you want?
- Lust energizes, but that's not the only thing that causes you to act out. What else motivates you?
- Are you angry at God?

Dig deep into his heart to expose the corrupt desires that have taken root there. As you pull out the roots, you expose what motivates him to seek out porn.

Our chief strategy as disciplers is to grow holy appetites in a sinner. *Holy appetites expel unholy desires.* As the addict grows in greater love for Christ, his affections drive out the weaker sexual desires.

That means we want to spend a significant portion of our time with sexual strugglers talking about Christ. We demonstrate that Christ really is the addict's hope by thinking about *who he is* and *what he done for us.* As much as we can, we marinate them in gospel truth. Because we come to know Christ through his Word, we spend time in the Word with the people we are discipling. And we make sure that strugglers are engaging the common means of grace (God's Word, prayer, fellowship with believers, consistent attendance at church, participation in the Lord's Supper).

Is most of your time focused on dealing with the addict's sin, or are you actively cultivating the addict's love for Christ? Do you point the addict to the common means of grace to grow her relationship with Christ? There is no better way to help a porn addict than to repeatedly set her eyes on the cross.

ATHEISM

Every believer wrestles with *momentary atheism*—she has occasions when she gives herself over to her unbelief. When Adelynn looks at porn, she chooses her sin over God. In that moment, she is embracing sin's lies, rebelling against God, and disbelieving the promises of the gospel. Viewing pornography is Adelynn's functional way of denying the existence of an all-loving God who has provided for her every need. It reveals her doubt regarding God's character—in terms of not just his love but also his mercy, goodness, and sovereignty over her life. In the moment that she acts out and looks at porn, she is declaring, "I believe the promises of my sin will satisfy me" and "I doubt the promises of God right now."

The struggler's momentary atheism leads to dangerous spiritual consequences. It's unlikely an addict will say, "I'm don't believe God's character or promises right now." He won't be that blunt. Rather, you'll witness firsthand the consequences of the atheism and porn struggles—a lack of assurance, a hard heart, and self-deceit. We've highlighted them for you below so you can look for them.

Lack of Assurance

Each time Adelynn views pornography, unbelief acts like a swarm of termites, eating away at the foundation of her faith. Questions plague her: "How can I profess to be a believer and doubt like this? How can I call myself a Christian and continue to look at porn and masturbate?" When Adelynn doubts, the apostle James tells us she's like "a wave of the sea that is driven and tossed by the wind" and is "double-minded . . . unstable in all [her] ways" (James 1:6, 8). This double-mindedness leaves her feeling unstable, even somewhat crazy. Doubt undermines her assurance as a believer. This doubt may be accompanied by a lack of engagement with the common means of grace. If an addict is not reading the Word (see Ps. 1:2), not pursuing regular fellowship with other believers or regularly attending church (see Heb. 10:25), not partaking in communion (see 1 Cor. 11:23–31), or not finding ways to love and serve others (see Mark 12:31; Gal. 5:13–14), her heart will grow cold to the Lord.

A Hard Heart

To embrace sin is to turn your back on the living God in unbelief. If tolerated and coddled, unbelief leads to a hardened heart. The author of Hebrews warns Christians, "Take care, brothers and sisters, lest there be in any of you an evil, unbelieving heart, leading you to fall away from the living God. But exhort one another every day . . . that none of you may be hardened by the deceitfulness of sin" (Heb. 3:12–13).

Imagine taking a hammer and slamming it down on a solid rock. It cracks a little, but the rock holds together. A hard heart is in a very dangerous place spiritually. What would it take to soften a hard heart (rather than chisel it!) and see it more open to Christ and the gospel?

As we see from Hebrews, a possible antidote to a hard heart is twofold. We have a personal responsibility to fight our unbelief: "take care . . . lest there be in any of you an evil, unbelieving heart" (v. 12). There is also help in daily fellowship with other believers: "exhort one another every day" (v. 13). These show us how to soften a heart, but they are also the preventative measures for slowing down the hardening of a Christian's heart.

Self-Deceit

Self-deceit starts early as the addict drifts away from God and the gospel. It doesn't happen by itself. Long before an addict acts out, self-deceit conspires with his desires (and sometimes his fears). A guy sees a girl in skimpy clothes on a hot spring day and begins to imagine the possibilities. He wants her. He wants sex. He wants to be affirmed. He buys into the lie: Jesus is not enough right now. As his heart rages and his body gets aroused, he can ignore his conscience and actively convince himself of anything. This is *the sin before the sin*. Self-deceit sets him on the well-worn pathway to acting out.

In a moment of self-deceit, the struggler doesn't want to see the truth or believe it. He doesn't want to believe that Christ is sufficient.

He *wants* pornography to satisfy him. Like the Pharisees who didn't want to believe Jesus was the Son of God, lest their Pharisaical house crumble (see John 12:19), so also an addict doesn't believe Christ is enough, lest he be forced to give up his sin. Sexual sin makes him feel good quickly, so he *wants* to believe it provides the relational satisfaction that he craves.[3] Is it any surprise that the devil wants us to question the One who is all-sufficient? The worst lies are the ones about the all-sufficient Christ.

This is the slippery path of a porn addiction—unbelief and rebellion lead to self-deceit, hardened hearts, and forsaking the Lord (see 1 Tim. 4:1). Practically speaking, you should encourage your struggling friend to take personal responsibility for fighting his doubts. As addictions get worse, believers can give up and give in.

But also take time to exhort your friend—to speak a gracious and loving but firm word. Ask him,

- Are you wrestling with doubts about God's character? If so, explain.
- Can you share some of your thoughts and feelings about God? (It may be embarrassing, especially if you've been critical of God in your thinking. But I encourage you to be honest.)
- Have you wrestled with any other kinds of doubts? If so, can you share them?
- Would you say your heart is hard or soft toward the gospel? What softens your heart?
- By its very nature, self-deceit is hard to recognize in yourself. So, let's consider: What do you get from your pornography habit? In what ways does your sin satisfy you? What are the promises of sin that you are believing? In contrast, are there promises of God that give you hope?

You may think, "I'm not going to make much of a difference." Who knows? Your words may be the very lifeline your friend needs to end his turning away from God and to persevere in his faith!

PUTTING IT ALL TOGETHER

The first two *As* (*access* and *anonymity*) deal with external temptations; the second two *As* (*appetite* and *atheism*) reveal the battle in the heart. When fighting sexual sin, we start with restricting access and anonymity. We take a radical approach to cutting off access points and getting rid of opportunities for anonymity.

Limiting open access and anonymity starves the appetite of our sinful nature. But this takes time. Change doesn't happen overnight. Addictions start early, are cultivated for years, and become ingrained as personal choices begin to rewrite our embodied existence. The longer the addiction has been cultivated, the longer it will take to get rid of it. Ingrained patterns take time to unwind. So be patient. Take a long-term view of starving the appetites of your friend's sinful nature.

But keep in mind that restricting access and anonymity alone is not an adequate strategy. An addict can cut off access to porn but still wrestle with fleshly desires that rage inside his heart and doubts that fill his mind. *At best, when you restrict access, you put a fortified wall around a sin-crazed heart.* When an addict develops good habits for fighting external temptations and achieves significant victory over them, the battle often shifts inward. Satan puts more pressure on the struggler's inner life—his appetites and atheism. The war in the heart becomes more fierce.

Consequently, our strategy shifts. Though we start by taking steps to limit access and anonymity, we then move to focusing on the internal war, in which the appetites of the heart are involved. As disciplers, we spend more time working through an addict's desires, motivations, and doubts than focusing on limiting access, as important as that is. At the same time, since issues with accessing porn and fighting off temptation consistently come up, we expect them to be a normal part of our conversations.

In this fight, it's a mistake to take a narrow view of a struggler and become far too focused on her sin. Faith is the wind in a sinner's sails. Without it, there is no true forward progress. Help her to fight unbelief, root out self-deceit, and grow in her affections for Christ.

Hold out to her the riches of our glorious Savior. After all, what better way to help a porn addict than to repeatedly set her eyes on the cross?

BUILD A RESCUE PLAN

Personal Reflection

Which of the four *A*s have you *least* addressed in your conversations with your friend who struggles with porn?

Potential Problems

If you entrust a struggler with shutting down the access points on his phone (or any other form of technology), often he'll fail to do so for days or weeks. Why? Laziness, pride, shame, self-condemnation, guilt, busyness. There is an endless list of reasons why a struggler delays and access points don't get shut down. So, we take initiative to shut down access points *in our meetings*. We say, "Pull out your phone and let's see how best to restrict your access."

If you do entrust the addict with shutting off access points on his own, get him to send you a text or email within forty-eight hours to confirm he got it done. That provides accountability for taking action sooner rather than later.

Practical Step

Spend time unraveling and correcting the self-deceit that partners with doubt. One way to do this is by exposing your friend's common lies and justifications for her sexual sin. Have your friend write out her lies and rationalizations for sin, share them with you, pray over them, and confess them to the Lord. Writing down the lies makes them more real and tangible and less slippery to the liar.

Prayer

Lord, help me to believe that you are more than sufficient for these things. In Jesus's name, amen!

PART 2

KNOW THE LAY OF THE LAND

The pressure was on—it was the morning of January 30, and the Rangers were set to commence their rescue at 7:30 p.m. that same day.[1] Scouts Bill Nellist and Tom Rounsaville had discovered that two hundred Japanese soldiers sat encamped in a bamboo grove about a mile northeast of the camp. And Cabanatuan City, four miles southwest of the prison camp, housed several thousand Japanese soldiers.[2] Any gunfighting or loud noises would attract the attention of these enemy soldiers and could easily throw the operation into disarray.

Unfortunately, the team still lacked adequate details about the camp itself.

Nellist had an idea. The Alamo scouts had been unable to get close enough to Cabantuan prison to collect the details they needed. Their scant information came from Filipino guerillas who pretended to be rice peasants and wandered around the camp's perimeter in straw hats and civilian clothes.

Nellist thought the scout team might be able to do something similar—they would don peasant costumes, walk up to a shack on stilts that stood near the prison, and try to view the camp from this elevated position.

Nellist and Filipino-American Private Rufo Vaquilar put on farmer disguises obtained by a Filipino runner, approached the shack at a distance of about a hundred feet from each other, and scurried up the ladder.[3]

Nellist fully expected the Japanese not to buy the ruse, but to his great surprise, the plan worked. As Nellist peered through the window that overlooked the camp, he saw the entire camp as clear as day—guards in watchtowers, American prisoners housed to the left, Japanese housed to the right, a building for the army's tanks, and much more.[4] The information they gained was exactly what Mucci and Prince needed to plan the operation.

In order to plan a successful operation, Mucci and his team needed to know where the enemy soldiers were located. They needed to know the lay of the land both inside and outside the prison.

In the war against pornography, we do something similar. Think of yourself as one of the Alamo scouts. You need to do reconnaissance—get a full understanding of everything that's going on in and around a prison of porn addiction. When it comes to the fight against pornography, masturbation and the role of key gender differences are included in the landscape.

Often porn problems and masturbation go together. We'll dedicate two chapters to the addictive habit of masturbation. To show our cards up front, we don't think masturbation fits with God's design for our sexuality, and we have five reasons why (chapter 4). But we won't leave you there. We'll also offer ten strategies that we've found to be effective for slowing down and stopping masturbation (chapter 5).

We'll also sort through how gender interacts with porn addictions. Most books treat pornography and masturbation as a man's struggle. From the male-only descriptions of sexual sin that you hear in pulpits to the way our culture talks about porn, women are left out. But women battle sexual sin too. So we'll consider how women are affected by sexual sin, what similarities and differences there are between men and women, and how knowledge of these gender specifics allows us to be more effective in our ministry to struggling believers (chapter 6).

4

MASTURBATION IS NOT WHAT GOD WANTS

Don't knock masturbation. It's sex with someone I love.
—*Woody Allen,* Annie Hall

It has occurred to me that masturbation
is the one great habit that is a "primary addiction."
—*Sigmund Freud,* The Origins of Psychoanalysis:
Letters to Wilhelm Fliess

Misery loves company. Sin often runs alongside sin. And pornography and masturbation typically go together. If you're discipling a man or a woman who is struggling with pornography, masturbation is the elephant in the room. You know that it's more than likely occurring. Whether you are helping young adolescents, singles, or married men and women, you'll need to address this issue.

Surveys show that 92 percent of males and 76 percent of females have masturbated.[1] Pastors rarely discuss masturbation, even though many in their congregations struggle with it. For older generations, masturbation is a taboo topic, especially within the church—but for younger generations, masturbation is considered a normal part of sexual development and exploration. To some, talking about the "dangers" of masturbation seems nonsensical because it is such an accepted part of life today.

Our goal in this brief chapter is to present a compelling case for why masturbation is not in keeping with God's design for healthy, thriving sexuality. However, before laying out our arguments *against* masturbation, we must consider the arguments *for* masturbation.

THE ARGUMENTS FOR MASTURBATION

Marcus looked at me (Jonathan) with a straight face as he quoted Ecclesiastes 9:1: "Whatever your hand finds to do, do it with all your might" (NIV). "You see? The Bible *does* talk about masturbation!" he exclaimed. Marcus's argument is a reminder that all of us have a tendency to read Scripture through our own lenses. It is quite easy to make Scripture say what you want it to say and to conveniently ignore other parts of it. Individuals who are looking for extrabiblical justification for masturbation do not have to look far:

- "The Bible never condemns masturbation!"
- "I'm not hurting anyone, so why is it bad?"
- "Everyone does it!"[2]
- "I don't want to cheat on my spouse, so this is a way for me to have an outlet for my sexual desires."
- "My husband can't give me an orgasm, so I need to do it on my own."
- "This is God's design for singles to give them a release without having premarital sex."
- "I can masturbate without having lustful thoughts."
- "I masturbate while thinking about my spouse. Surely that isn't wrong."

These arguments and others have gained popular traction amongst evangelicals in recent years due to several different factors. One factor is the pro-masturbation messages Christians receive from Christian leaders on this topic. Plenty of evangelical leaders argue that the Bible is silent on masturbation. Therefore, they say, masturbation is morally neutral and biblically permissible.[3] Pastor and author Tim Chester writes, "Because the Bible doesn't address masturbation explicitly, we should be cautious about giving a blanket condemnation."[4] *Christianity Today* columnist Tim Stafford adds, "The Bible isn't shy about mentioning sex, but masturbation is never referred to. I think the very least you can conclude is that masturbation isn't the most important issue in the world from God's perspective."[5]

Fascinatingly, some of the most vocal opponents of masturbation have been non-Christians. Jean-Jacques Rousseau called masturbation "the most deadly habit to which a young man can be subject," and Immanuel Kant described masturbation as people giving themselves over to "animal inclinations."[6]

James Dobson, a well-known clinical psychologist and Christian figure, promotes the view that masturbation is a physiological issue that is morally neutral as long as one can keep it from the realm of lust.[7] Dobson does not view masturbation as a sin or lust issue: "I believe the best way to prevent [teens from masturbating] is for adults not to emphasize or condemn it. Regardless of what you do, you will not stop the practice of masturbation in your teenagers. That is a certainty. You'll just drive it underground. . . . Nothing works as a 'cure.'"[8]

A second factor is the way people in a post-Christian culture evaluate right and wrong, good and bad. Instead of forming our moral convictions on moral absolutes given to us by God, we now make our moral convictions based off our gut feelings. Psychologist Jonathan Haidt calls these gut feelings *moral taste buds*. Does a given course of action seem harmful or not? Freeing or oppressive? Fair or discriminatory? These primary factors, Haidt argues, determine our conclusions about whether something is right or wrong.[9]

This faulty threefold test explains the dilemma that many pastors, counselors, and disciplers encounter when talking to men and women about masturbation.

- *Is it harmful or not?* Whether I masturbate or don't masturbate doesn't hurt anyone, so it must be okay.
- *Is it freeing or oppressive?* Why would you limit my personal freedom? What I do in the privacy of my own home is my business.

- *Is it fair or discriminatory?* It seems pretty arbitrary and unfair to prohibit masturbation.

After using the *moral taste buds* test to process the question of whether or not masturbation is right or wrong, many individuals come out convinced that masturbation is fully in accord with God's ethic and plan for sexuality.

WHY CHRISTIANS SHOULD NOT MASTURBATE

Does the absence of an explicit mention of masturbation in the Bible mean that Scripture does not speak to this issue? We'll argue that unless a Christian can find a Scripture passage that explicitly permits sexual expression and gratification outside marriage, the de facto position is to live within the healthy boundaries that God has created for sex within marriage.[10] Because of what Jesus says about sexual immorality and its effects on the soul, the stakes are too high for us to take any other position.

We hold to God's boundaries of sexual expression within marriage. Thus, our argument goes against typical evangelical (and, of course, cultural) thinking. Chester, Dobson, and Haidt each show us a different aspect of why Christians argue *for* masturbation. They show what we're up against.

How should you approach the topic of masturbation? What are you going to say when this comes up? Consider five reasons why Christians should refrain from masturbation.

Reason 1: Masturbation Goes against the Creator's Design for Sexuality

In his Word, the Lord provides an overarching framework for how we are to view sexuality and our bodies. If we remember God's overall intention and design for sex, then we see that fitting masturbation into that paradigm is highly problematic.

God's design for sex. The passages below provide a framework of how to think about sexuality from God's perspective. Consider working through these passages with your struggling friend to evaluate whether or not he or she believes masturbation is in keeping with this design:

- Genesis 2:24–25: God describes the one-flesh union between husband and wife.
- Matthew 5:27–30: Jesus reminds us that lust in the heart is equated with adultery.
- Romans 12:1–2: In response to our salvation and in light of God's mercies, we dedicate our bodies and minds to the Lord.
- 1 Corinthians 7:1–5: Paul describes who has authority over the body in a marriage relationship.
- 2 Corinthians 10:5: We are called to take every thought captive in order to obey Christ.
- 1 Thessalonians 4:1–8: God's will is for our sexual holiness and purity. Self-control and abstinence are fruits of the Spirit-filled life.

God is the great Creator, and he gave us sex as a gift. He didn't have to make a way for us to be intimate that's so pleasurable, but he did. The Creator's design is for sex to be enjoyed within a covenant marriage between a man and a woman. The Lord gives sex to a couple *together*.

What's the point of God's gift of sex? It is certainly for a couple's pleasure. It's also for procreation—to make babies! In addition, God uses sexual intimacy to foster unity in marriage. When sexual intimacy is done right, the uniting power of sex can be a true balm to couples. Intimacy strengthens a couple's relationship during times of trial, difficulty, and hardship. It reinforces their covenant commitment as well as provides opportunities for mutual vulnerability and affirmation.

Fitting masturbation into God's design for sex. If God's purpose for sex is aimed at helping two to become one, masturbation seems to do the exact opposite. It selfishly feeds *one* individual and robs the husband and wife as a *couple*. It confuses our hearts as our desires are channeled in the wrong direction (toward ourselves), and it muddies God's greater purposes for sex.

Imagine it's a bright sunny day and I (Deepak) am standing at Nationals Park, ready to take my turn to swing at a pitch. I walk up to the plate, and almost immediately I notice that the catcher, the umpire, and the entire opposing team are looking at me funny. Rather than standing there with a baseball bat, I am holding my black Nike sneaker in my hand. What would you think? You'd say to me, "A sneaker won't work. You're supposed to use a baseball bat." If you mix up the functional purpose of something—you misunderstand what it's supposed to be used for—then you look silly, don't you? If you use a sneaker as a baseball bat, you don't understand the purpose of a sneaker and the point of a baseball bat. And you become the worst batter in the history of Major League Baseball!

The same thing applies to masturbation. When we masturbate, we settle for an inadequate substitute rather than patiently wait to experience God's good design (sex with a spouse within marriage). We discard God's holy purposes for marriage and instead exalt our selfish desires.

Miguel and Irene didn't prioritize marital intimacy because of busyness. That left Miguel feeling ignored and overlooked by his wife. He created excuses to masturbate ("I've got needs—doesn't she know that?") and started to masturbate when she wasn't around. He confessed to me (Deepak), "I don't like it. It feels like I'm eating cotton candy for a sugar high." He could sense how deficient masturbation was compared to marital intercourse.

God created sex and sexuality not primarily for our individual pleasure but to bring him glory. As you stare at the contrast between covenanted sex and masturbation, what do you find? Masturbation feels like cotton candy, and the Lord is offering you a juicy four-pound T-bone steak. Masturbation is a quick fix, when what's intended for you is much more profound and glorious.

Please note—we're *not* trying to get rid of your sexual desire. Sexual desire should be directed toward healthy and holy purposes so you end up with a satisfying relationship with your spouse.[11] If you're not married and desire to be, you can wait on the Lord and rely on his strength to fight for purity, praying for a day when the Lord will allow you to express intimacy in marriage.

"Mutual sacrificial self-giving love for the good of the other by a husband and wife: every word in that formula matters. It's not a complete statement about the shape of Christian teaching about sexual ethics . . . but when thinking through [masturbation] it gets you a long ways toward seeing why [masturbation] undermines marital and personal flourishing." —**Matthew Lee Anderson**[12]

Reason 2: Masturbation Is Self-Centered and Self-Oriented

Masturbation is solo sex—it's when a person stimulates himself or herself to orgasm without the involvement of another person. It's *self*-arousal for the sake of *self*-pleasure. By its nature, masturbation has an inherently *self*-focused and *self*-satisfying quality to it. Professor and author Stuart Scott explains that as a believer, you are "not [to] use your own body to gratify yourself. . . . This act is clearly not the right use of our intimate parts. Our bodies are not meant to serve us, but God and our wife (see 1 Cor. 7:4; 1 Cor. 13:5)."[13] Masturbation feeds our carnal cravings for sexual desire when, in fact, God calls us to holiness (see 1 Peter 1:15–16), purity (see 1 Tim. 5:1–2), service of others (see Phil. 2:3–4), and love (see 1 John 3:16). Masturbation is all about *me*. It's preoccupied with gratifying my sexual needs rather than showing selfless love to others.

There may be a place for a husband or wife to help his or her spouse to reach orgasm in the context of marital lovemaking without vaginal intercourse. For example, if a wife is unable to have vaginal intercourse for a period of time, she can stimulate her husband to orgasm through a number of other sexually intimate acts. Thus, when we speak of masturbation in this chapter, we're using the term to refer to independent acts apart from a spouse.

Biblical love is concerned for the well-being of others at a cost to self.[14] The apostle proclaims, "In humility count others more significant than [yourself]" (Phil. 2:3–4) and tells us that love "is not self-seeking" (1 Cor. 13:5 NIV). Masturbation runs antithetical to this kind of love because it revolves around *me*. Masturbation's mantra is "Look to your own interests, not to the interests of others, so you can satisfy yourself with pleasure."

To summarize, masturbation turns the focus on *my* needs and *my* wants. Other people, if involved at all (even in a pornographic manner), are used as a means to an end. There is no covenant relationship. There is no self-giving love for the good and pleasure of another. Masturbation is antithetical to biblical love. It is so self-focused that we can't see how it does a person any good.

Reason 3: Masturbation Inhibits a Believer's Relationship with the Lord

What have we learned so far? Masturbation does not fit with God's overall design for sexuality and flourishing, and it is ultimately self-focused and self-oriented. Let's add another vital point: masturbation hurts and hinders a believer's relationship with the Lord.

Take a glance at these texts:

Blessed are the pure in heart, for they shall see God. (Matt. 5:8)

Put on the Lord Jesus Christ, and make no provisions for the flesh, to gratify its desires. (Rom. 13:14)

Put to death therefore what is earthly in you: sexual immorality, impurity, passion, evil desire, and covetousness, which is idolatry. On account of these the wrath of God is coming. (Col. 3:5–6)

It is God's will that you should be sanctified: that you should avoid sexual immorality. (1 Thess. 4:3 NIV)

Abstain from the passions of the flesh, which wage war against your soul. (1 Peter 2:11)

What does the devil want? He wants a believer to be preoccupied with his flesh and distracted from loving the Lord. He wants the porn struggler to spend his evenings thinking more about sex and less about Jesus. He wants a Christian's passions to be enflamed so that he feels overwhelmed and helpless in his fight against sexual sin. Here's the devil's dirty little secret: A believer can't stay close to God and develop a passion for the Lord's glory while simultaneously indulging his selfish fleshly desires. They're mutually exclusive. Satan wants the Christian to be preoccupied with his flesh. In that way, the Evil One keeps a Christian away from God. Is your friend playing into Satan's manipulative plans?

Masturbation significantly increases feelings of guilt and shame. And we know that the ashamed and guilty run away from the One who offers to meet them in their time of need. How can an experience like masturbation be morally neutral? If you push people, we believe that deep down inside, the vast majority will recognize that masturbation *does not* bring them closer to God but instead pushes them further away.

For many, masturbation turns into an alternate refuge, a place to escape to find self-fulfillment and pleasure. It's a false paradise that offers quick fixes to a person's sexual cravings. It's a shortcut around the long, hard, patient work of serving the Lord with every aspect of life. Masturbation distracts us from centering our lives on Christ. We run to it for immediate gratification rather than enduring suffering and turning to the Lord as our rock, fortress, and refuge (see Ps. 46:1–3, 11).[15]

Reason 4: Masturbation Is Enslaving

Masturbation enslaves. It imprisons. As with other addictions, there is a choice involved, but masturbation also involves a strong component of compulsivity. Many individuals who struggle with masturbation speak of their desire to stop while acknowledging how difficult it is to break the cycle of fantasy and indulgence.

Although promising pleasure and freedom, masturbation eventually enslaves a person to her own desires (see 1 Cor. 6:12). While sex

within marriage offers honor and freedom (see Heb. 13:4), masturbation offers imprisonment. Writing to a friend, author C. S. Lewis
describes how this happens:

> For me the real evil of masturbation [would] be that it takes an
> appetite which, in lawful use, leads the individual out of himself
> to complete (and correct) his own personality in that of another
> (and finally in children and even grandchildren) and turns it back:
> sends the man back into the prison of himself, there to keep a
> harem of imaginary brides. And this harem, once admitted, works
> against his *ever* getting out and really uniting with a real woman.
> . . . Among those shadowy brides he is always adored, always the
> perfect lover: no demand is made on his unselfishness, no mortifi-
> cation ever imposed on his vanity. In the end, they become merely
> the medium through which he increasingly adores himself. . . .
> After all, almost the *main* work of life is to *come out* of ourselves,
> out of the little, dark prison we are all born in. Masturbation is to
> be avoided as *all* things are to be avoided [that] retard this process.
> The danger is that of coming to *love* the prison.[16]

According to Lewis, masturbation sends an individual back to
the prison of self, not to the service of another. It runs antithetical to Christianity, which calls us to come out of the prison of our
self-serving erotic desires and to submit them (and everything in our
lives) to the Lord.

As we mentioned in the last section, when believers masturbate,
guilt and shame often follow and become the walls of a prison. The
strugglers experience self-condemnation. They have a sense of failure
over giving in to the temptation yet again. They are ashamed of their
inability to control their passions. They may be embarrassed about
exposing their foolishness to others and become overly concerned
with other people's opinions. Those addicted to masturbation find
themselves trapped in a horrible loop of fantasy and indulgence, guilt
and shame.

Reason 5: Masturbation Runs Contrary to the Biblical Call for Self-Control

Masturbation feeds our fleshly desires. It stokes our desire for more. Its cravings are never satisfied. It *always* wants more.

As Christians, we're called to self-control (see 1 Tim. 2:9, 15; 3:2; Titus 1:8; 2:2, 5–6; 2 Peter 1:6).[17] We are exhorted to discipline our bodies (see 1 Cor. 9:25–27) and to use them to glorify God (see 1 Cor. 6:19–20). We are to restrain ourselves in the realm of sex (see Prov. 25:28; 1 Cor. 7:1–2; Gal. 5:22–23; 1 Thess. 4:3–6; 2 Tim. 1:7). Self-control and "every form of self-denial can function as a spiritual discipline, nurturing one's dependence on God and helping a person find one's satisfaction in God (1 Corinthians 9:26–27; 1 Timothy 4:7–8). Denying the body's cravings to masturbate can develop greater surrender to the control of the Spirit (Romans 8:13; Galatians 5:16)."[18]

Masturbation skirts around and removes any need for a person to exercise self-control in the arena of sex. That's dangerous because it takes only a little hole to sink an entire ship. A person who downplays the problem of masturbation is treating it like that little hole. A person may think, "Masturbation is not a big deal," but believers should take seriously the Bible's charge—found all throughout Scripture—for them to be self-controlled with their desires and lusts, thoughts and bodies.

A person might argue, "I *can't* restrain myself. I continue to burn with passion. So why can't I use masturbation to satisfy my bodily urges and my sexual desires?" A believer should not give in to the lie that he can't control his sexual passions. Scripture says it *is* possible to live a self-controlled life. The Lord is not going to leave a believer to fight this battle on his own.[19] If the Bible says the only permissible options are marriage or self-control, not masturbation, then the Lord will help a struggler not to masturbate. God's power is available to him. God *will* strengthen a believer for this fight. (If you're not sure how to fight against masturbation, hold tight. In the next chapter, we'll discuss the God-given means of fighting sexual sin.)

75

CONCLUSION

As we look over these biblical arguments against masturbation, we must help our friends to place their faith and trust in the Lord's goodness. God creates boundaries around a Christian's life, including his sexuality (see 1 Thess. 4:3). Believers must trust the Lord, who knows and seeks our best. God is not trying to hide something from his children. He's not being mean. He loves those who are his own. He is good and righteous, just and true, and wise in all his ways. The Evil One stands next to us and whispers, "Satisfy your desires. Don't listen to God's Word. Masturbation is not that big a deal. Just enjoy yourself and move on. Tomorrow it won't matter." As helpers, we must speak truthfully and compassionately to our friends who struggle with masturbation. We must be determined not to let the Evil One get the final word, especially since we know that God will continue to strengthen and sustain his children in this fight.

BUILD A RESCUE PLAN

Personal Reflection

What's your personal practice regarding masturbation? (What you do will often be passed on to those whom you disciple.) What biblical argument against masturbation is most persuasive to you, and why? Or are you not sure how to think about masturbation? Do you believe God will give your friend the strength to persevere in purity and holiness?

Potential Problems

A believer can get to a place where he or she no longer (or rarely) accesses pornography but still masturbates often. Because masturbation continues to feed the fleshly desires (see Rom. 13:14), it strengthens the struggler's greedy cravings for more.

Practical Step

Discuss the five reasons in this chapter with the friend you are discipling and take time to pray together. If your friend is not convinced, don't rush to condemnation. Be patient, pray, and continue to talk over this together.

Prayer

Lord, grant me wisdom and tactfulness as I speak. Help me to be clear and biblical, truthful and gracious. Help me to lean into areas of conversation that may be difficult and uncomfortable, and give me your strength, your power, your words, and your compassion. In Jesus's name, amen!

5

TEN STRATEGIES TO ADDRESS MASTURBATION

*Take responsibility for your sin, trusting that God will forgive
and cleanse you because of his faithfulness, not yours.*
—*Winston Smith,* The Problem with Masturbation

*The Christian life, the spiritual life, is not about
information or getting things done. It's about living.*
—*Eugene Peterson, "A Conversation with
Eugene Peterson" (with Luci Shaw)*

In the last chapter, we laid out a biblical case for why masturbation is
not in line with God's intention for a flourishing human sexuality. In
this chapter, we'll give you practical tools for helping your friend to
battle masturbation. This battle can be discouraging, especially if the
struggler has become enslaved to this habit. As you read this chapter,
keep the following in mind.

A believer's obedience is accomplished not by his own willpower
but by God's work in him. Whenever Scripture exhorts believers to
work out their salvation, it's asking them to obey and to do what's
right—but it doesn't root their ability to defeat sin in their own mea-
ger willpower. What does the apostle Paul say? "Work out your own
salvation with fear and trembling, for it is God who works in you,
both to will and to work for his good pleasure" (Phil. 2:12–13). Paul
says, "You can obey *because God is working in you*." It should comfort
us that we're not on our own in this fight.

With God's help, it's possible for your friend to overcome sexual temptations and not give in to the urge to masturbate. Through Christ, God gives believers the strength they need for this fight (see Mark 10:27). When the apostle Paul tells Christians to say no to ungodliness and worldly lusts, he roots their self-control and ability to say no in "the grace of God" that "train[s] us" and "Jesus Christ who gave himself for us to redeem us" and "to purify for himself a people for his own possession who are zealous for good works" (Titus 2:11–14). Christ purchased the power we need for our sexual purity.[1] A Christian's self-control is a fruit of the Spirit (see Gal. 5:23)—a supernatural work of God in him through Christ. That should give believers hope that they can restrain the passions that motivate masturbation. Is Christ sufficient to give a believer self-control and restraint from her passions? Yes, he is.

STRATEGY 1: GUARD YOUR HEART

Solomon writes, "Above all else, guard your heart, for everything you do flows from it" (Prov. 4:23 NIV). For some people, the phrase *guard your heart* carries with it connotations of resisting any sort of romantic or sexual feelings about another person. The phrase became a staple of purity culture in the early 1990s. We don't want misunderstandings associated with this phrase or a '90s dating culture to obscure Scripture's teaching.

Scripture teaches that your heart is the command center in which your deeper motivations reside and from which flow your thoughts, feelings, words, and actions (see Matt. 12:33–37; Luke 6:43–45). Solomon tells us in Proverbs 4 to be watchful and vigilant over our hearts because that's where our lives start.

We must come alongside believers and help them to be vigilant in protecting their hearts and lives from the sin of masturbation and the guilt and shame that often come from it. How does someone guard his or her heart?

Explore the Deeper Motivations

Axel called me (Deepak) and confessed that he had masturbated. When I asked him what had happened, he explained. It had been his thirtieth birthday. He'd enjoyed a birthday dinner with friends, but when he'd gotten home, he'd started dwelling on the fact that he was thirty and not married yet. The longer he contemplated this, the sadder he became. His ensuing tailspin of self-pity culminated with his looking at images online and masturbating.

Was lust involved in this incident? Absolutely. Was it *only* about lust? Not at all. If you pressed further, you'd find that soon after he started to feel sorry for himself, the justifications for sin rolled in through the door of his heart: "God hasn't given you a wife. You deserve something for your misery." There were deeper motivations behind his sin, and Axel needed to understand the war in his own heart.

Motivations—the goals and desires that define our lives—reside within the heart. As disciplers, we help Axel by asking heart-oriented questions that draw out deeper issues and promote greater self-awareness. Solomon's Proverbs 4:23 goal is for Axel to guard his heart from self-pity and masturbation. Normally, that means heading off both early on. But if Axel acts out, it may mean helping him to figure out what went wrong so that we can prevent it from happening again.

In Axel's case, we ask, "What happened before you acted out?" If his answer is just a behavior ("I went home and lay in bed for a long time"), we get him to explore his thoughts and feelings, which reveal the state of his heart. "What were you thinking and feeling before you masturbated?" "What kinds of rationalizations did you come up with to justify your sin?" The goal is not only to help Axel to grow in greater self-awareness but also to challenge him to consider where he needs to repent.

Avoid Danger Zones and Know the Exits

When a person identifies the places where, and times when, she most commonly struggles with masturbation (for example, late at night while lying in bed; after lingering in the shower too long), she can make conscious attempts to avoid those situations or make adjustments that set her mind on more edifying things.

Far too often, when we ask a person what she does when she faces temptation, she answers, "I don't know." If a believer doesn't know what exit strategies she can employ to fight her sin, she'll consistently get in trouble. It behooves you and your friend to take time to work out specific exit strategies for troubling moments. Brainstorm. Talk about what's worked in the past. Try new things. Make sure she walks into moments of temptation knowing what escape hatch to access when carnal desires overtake her heart.

- Bobby took quick showers rather than lingering. He knew that if he hung out in the shower too long, he'd eventually masturbate.
- Shannon sought accountability for her intake of sexually explicit romance novels. Over the past year, she'd often given in to the temptation to masturbate. She knew her diet of entertainment was feeding feelings of loneliness, jealousy, and discontent, so she went cold turkey and cut them out of her life.
- Clarence knew if he lay awake for a while, he'd struggle with the temptation to masturbate. If he felt trapped in bed late at night and was having a hard time sleeping, he'd flip on the light and read his Bible until he was tired.
- When Candace felt tempted to masturbate, she'd go on a long run.

Exercise Self-Control and Self-Denial

A person can pursue self-control in several ways: by adjusting daily routines, forming new habits, guarding his or her eyes, putting devices out of reach when he or she is vulnerable, and disciplining his or her mind. Practical steps can be taken to develop a regular practice of protecting the heart from the junk that wants to take over.

- Peter disciplines his eyes not to linger on the bodies he sees on the street or on a phone or computer screen; if a scantily clad woman walks by, he turns his eyes away.

- Amira restrains her mind and heart from dwelling on images stored up in her brain. She verbalizes her need for self-restraint in her self-talk ("I need to stop dwelling on these images. Through Christ I can do this"). If that doesn't slow down her thinking, she either reaches out for help from a friend or distracts herself so she doesn't dwell on the images.
- Todd describes his attempt to exercise self-control this way: "I put my phone on a charger outside my room at night. The temptation isn't as readily available, and I'm inconvenienced by the time it takes to get up and walk across multiple rooms to get my phone. During that time, the weight of my sin and the realization of what I am giving in to typically affect my decision and lead me to praying in repentance and crying for help."

STRATEGY 2: FILL YOUR HEART

Human beings not only think but also desire and worship. Therefore, it is not enough to occasionally think right thoughts about the Lord. To survive the battle with sexual sin, a struggler needs to fill his heart and imagination with a vision of who God is. He must train his whole being to be oriented to Christ.

Typical catalysts for arousal and masturbation are the images stored up in a struggler's mind. After years of engaging with pornography, a person has created and cataloged a storehouse of mental images. Unfortunately, these images are easily and readily accessible. Many strugglers experience frustration and discouragement, because although they are refraining from seeking out pornography, they still recall pornographic images that lead them to masturbate. That was the case for my (Jonathan's) friend Todd.

Remember that the battle for sanctification is wide, long, and deep.[2] Those memories are there, but they don't have to *stay* there. Through the power of the Holy Spirit, Todd can consecrate his mind and set it on things above! Paul writes in Romans 12:2, "Do not be conformed to this world, but *be transformed by the renewal of your mind.*" This transformation is a joint effort between a believer and the Spirit. As a discipler, this is what I (Jonathan) said to Todd: "Engage the Spirit; be filled with the Spirit. Remind yourself of what is truly beautiful and worthy of your mental attentiveness, and fill your mind with those images." Here are a few examples we discovered in Scripture and worked through together:

- Exodus 15:1–8: The Lord goes before his people and mightily fights on their behalf.
- Psalm 18:1–2: The Lord is a rock, fortress, and deliverer in whom we can take refuge.
- Psalm 121:1–2: We can lift our eyes to the Lord and cry out to him for help.
- Isaiah 40:12–15: The Lord holds the waters of the world in the palm of his hand.

These and other images of the Lord and his work in creation can and should motivate a believer's heart to worship. As these images sink deep into Todd's soul, he creates a better storehouse of images and truths to draw from in times of temptation.

Todd told me that evening was his most difficult time to maintain purity. When he would go to bed, his mind would wander through his mental catalog of explicit images. If he didn't fall asleep quickly, he would dwell on illicit mental images and then masturbate. I began working with him to adjust his evening routine and overall schedule. He cut out media in the evenings, but that was just a start. To fill his heart with better things, he made a practice of reading a psalm and journaling before bed. That set his focus on worshipping the Lord before he went to sleep. Slowly and surely, his struggle grew less intense.

Three scriptural encouragements shape this exercise:

I have set the LORD always before me;
> because he is at my right hand, I shall not be shaken. (Ps.
> 16:8)

One thing have I asked of the L_ORD_,
    that will I seek after:
that I may dwell in the house of the L_ORD_
    all the days of my life,
to gaze upon the beauty of the L_ORD_
    and to inquire in his temple. (Ps. 27:4)

Finally, brothers and sisters, whatever is true, whatever is honorable, whatever is just, whatever is pure, whatever is lovely, whatever is commendable, if there is any excellence, if there is anything worthy of praise, think about these things. (Phil. 4:8)

Encourage your struggling friends to find practical ways to set the Lord always before them, such as by reading, journaling, singing, praying, and memorizing Scripture. Are there ways to engage their senses of sight, smell, touch, and hearing to draw their hearts to the Lord? Are there ways they can journal, draw, or experience creation to fan the flames of their affections for the Lord? How can you encourage them to gaze on the beauty of the Lord?[3]

STRATEGY 3: DON'T NARROW YOUR FOCUS TO A TIMELINE

People get obsessed with timelines when it comes to pornography and masturbation. Typically, a struggler (like our friend Michaela) tells us something like, "I've gone two weeks without masturbating or viewing porn." In this way, she narrows the entire process of sanctification down to a timeframe rather than a holistic approach.

What do we mean? Let's say that the two-week period of abstinence was porn-free but the struggler's disordered desires got directed somewhere else—to video gaming, gambling, eating, exercising excessively, or abusing alcohol. Would we say that two-week period represents growth? Probably not.

Too often a hyper-focus on timelines creates significant problems when those timelines and thresholds get broken. As disciplers, we can put too much emphasis on *how long* a person is pure and act as though victory centers on the struggler's achieving certain numerical goals. A struggler can feel like a failure when she rarely achieves certain goals. Timelines create too narrow a focus and won't promote growth and change.

What *should* be the struggler's focus? Let's look at strategy 4.

STRATEGY 4: EMPHASIZE THE STRUGGLER'S RELATIONSHIP WITH CHRIST

Sanctification is an overall life trajectory of change in Christ. What kind of change are we looking for? Are we looking to see someone become just a porn-free, non-masturbating person? No! We are looking for believers who are growing day by day into the image of Christ in *every* area of their lives.

Michaela "messed up" with pornography after a monthlong fast and ended up binging on pornography all weekend. When questioned by her discipler, Judy, she said, "I had already messed up my progress, so I figured I should just get it all out of my system before I started again." The thinking goes like this: "I know I'll need to confess and repent after this, so I may as well let myself go and *then* ask God to forgive me." Some have called it the *"what the hell" effect*—a defeatist attitude that allows for indulgence: "I failed, so I may as well enjoy it."

Friend, this ungodly thinking and defeatist attitude must be addressed, refuted, and corrected. What does Paul say in Romans 6?

> What shall we say then? Are we to continue in sin that grace may abound? By no means! How can we who died to sin still live in it? Do you not know that all of us who have been baptized into Christ Jesus were baptized into his death? (vv. 1–3)

The apostle Paul anticipates the arguments of his opponents. They will say that because Paul has emphasized justification through free grace, believers will consider this a license to sin. Paul tells us that we can't ever presume on God's grace and say, "It's fine to sin because

God will forgive me." That's cheap grace. Our forgiveness came at the great cost of Christ's blood! A believer recognizes that she is dead to sin and can no longer live in it (see Rom. 6:2).

Our conversations with Michaela helped her to grow in awareness of her sin while avoiding a hyper-focus on timelines and a defeatist attitude after her hard falls. In light of God's grace and her union with Christ, Michaela could pursue holiness, live in purity, and take advantage of God's grace by not continuing in her pattern of sin.

Although Michaela went on to experience a few weeks of freedom, her discipler, Judy, knew she wasn't in a place where they could stop the conversation. She asked Michaela the following questions that focused on her *relationship* with the Lord:

- Do you have an increased sense of gratitude to the Lord for all things in your life?
- Are you increasing your dependence on the Lord through prayer? Are you seeking him for wisdom?
- In what practical ways are you loving and serving your spouse? Your kids? Your coworkers? Your neighbors? Your enemies?
- How do you respond when things don't go your way?
- Do you see how your sin hurts your relationship with the Lord?

It was this last question that stirred Michaela's Spirit-driven conviction. She realized that her goal was not just to get rid of her sin but to see her sin in light of Christ. She began to experience a shift in her disposition toward the Lord:

> The turning point in my struggle with sexual sin, after repentance, was an understanding of how my sin truly did affect Christ and my relationship with him. My sin was not self-contained, nor was the most affected person my spouse. Sinning against Jesus is the worst part about this, and he's the one who matters the most. I'm not glorifying him when I masturbate. Although it's worthwhile to be concerned about the effects I have on my marriage and spouse, they are not the ultimate reason for me to resist my sexual sin.

I need to repent of my sexual sin because it hurts my relationship with Christ. I need to turn back to my Savior.

The gospel interrupts a narrow focus on timelines and defeatist attitudes. As the Spirit convicts a struggling person, he shifts her gaze toward Christ. This is where a Christian must focus. This is where she must put her concerted energies. This is what she's called to believe—that Christ's death and resurrection are sufficient for her in her struggle. Michaela's plight is not beyond Jesus's attention or power. The author of Hebrews sums it up: "Let us also lay aside . . . sin which clings so closely, and let us run with endurance the race that is set before us, looking to Jesus, the founder and perfecter of our faith, who for the joy that was set before him endured the cross, despising the shame" (Heb. 12:1–2). Michaela realized that she was called to run a race, and in that race her focus ought to be on the face of Jesus Christ, not her timeline.

The race is about much more than just fighting masturbation. It is a matter of trusting Christ daily as an entire way of life. Michaela casts aside *every* sin that clings to her and runs the race with endurance. She perseveres through daily trials and temptations by looking to Jesus, who is the author and finisher of her faith. Because Jesus endured the cross for her sake, Michaela can run her race with confidence.

The best way to fight masturbation is to have a vibrant relationship with Christ. It's not a strategy; it's an entire way of life. That's what we want for Michaela—for her to run her race with her eyes fixed on Christ.

STRATEGY 5: THINK ABOUT THE AFTERMATH OF MASTURBATION

An older man once told me (Jonathan) that sin will take you farther than you want to go and keep you there longer than you want to stay. That rings true, doesn't it? Although sin initially seems so promising, in the aftermath we often find that it was out of control.

That's why it's so helpful to think through the consequences before we engage in sin. Author Matt Fradd writes, "Finish the fantasy. This might sound counterintuitive, but it is so practical. . . . Picture yourself following through with the action—walking to your computer, binging on porn for a few hours, masturbating, and then feeling like a miserable failure. . . . [This] pushes us past the feeling of anticipation and the rush of excitement to the reality."[4]

Here are some of the ways people have described how and what they felt post-masturbation:

- Intense guilt over falling again
- Shame over struggling with the same sin again and again
- Regret over breaking a "timeline of good behavior"
- A sense of being dirty, perverted, used, and unworthy
- A sense of being a burden to others, including their disciplers, their friends, their accountability partners, and their spouses
- A sense of having disappointed and let down loved ones in their lives
- Loss of assurance of their salvation
- A temptation to give up because the struggle is never going to get better

What are conspicuously absent from the sentiments above? Positive feelings of growth and hope. A Christian has never come in after viewing pornography and masturbating and told us, "Yeah, I feel really good about myself! God's really at work in my life right now!"

Solomon writes, "Good understanding gives favor; the way of sinners is hard" (Prov. 13:15, author's translation). A person who has keen insight into her dilemma will receive favor. Her insight will aid her in her life. In contrast, sinners lack insight, and their lives are therefore much harder. Solomon adds, "There is a way that seems right to a man, but its end is the way to death" (Prov. 14:12). Solomon refers to the difference between perception and reality. A person thinks he's headed down the right path. He listens to sin's promises ("You'll feel good if you masturbate. You'll enjoy the pleasure!") and thinks, "That's what I want." Alas, he's blind to the end—the way of death. The reality is that his sin will end in misery.

The end of our sin is always death and destruction (see James 1:13–15). This is the great exchange of Satan—he promises life, but he delivers enslavement and death. Helping the struggler to discuss this can be a helpful teaching opportunity. Help your friend not to lose sight of where his sin will take him. Envisioning the end of his sin can inform his present actions and give him just enough hesitation to slow him down. Ask thoughtful questions, such as "After falling into temptation, how do you feel?" or "How do you feel about your relationship with the Lord?"

STRATEGY 6: BE AWARE OF YOUR TRIGGERS

Sexual desire may be stoked by *obvious* triggers (for example, an image of a naked man or woman)[5] and by *less obvious* triggers (like getting frustrated or mad at your boss or spouse).[6] It is wise for a struggling believer to grow in his awareness of the triggers that provoke his flesh. This allows him to avoid what he can (like salacious images online or porn websites) and to be sensitive to what he cannot (conflict in the office or in his marriage). With greater awareness of his triggers, he can make plans for how to respond well when they show up, as we saw in Strategy 1, "Guard Your Heart."

Triggers may include, but are not limited to, the following:

- High amounts of sensory stimulation (television / Internet / social media consumption)
- Desire for stimulation in order to "feel something"
- Conflict, disunity, and disconnection from a spouse or loved one
- Memories of sexual abuse, trauma, or sexual dysfunction
- Travel times away from a spouse
- Extended periods of time alone
- Physical and emotional discomfort
- Certain smells, sounds (for example, music or song lyrics), or locations that are reminders of past sexual situations
- Unhealthy consumption of alcohol or other substances that numb and limit a person's self-control

STRATEGY 7: PERFORM A LIFE AUDIT

Normally the word *audit* strikes fear in our hearts. The kind of audit we are looking for isn't tax related (go ahead, breathe a sigh of relief!) but related to how a struggler structures his entire life. Pastors, counselors, and helpers can help by offering strugglers a number of tools for tracking their use of time:

- Are there any time-sucking applications on their phones they need to consider removing and deleting?
- Can they track their screen time on their smartphones?
- Can they track their daily schedules for a week and bring it to you the next time you meet with them?
- Can they list any and all entertainment subscriptions they currently have?
- How do they spend their discretionary time? With friends? On hobbies? Sports? Service opportunities?

Evaluating how the struggler spends his time begins to shed light on what he values. It can also help you to identify how certain time-management issues lead the struggler to fall into temptation.

- Hunter realizes that extensive time at his local gym can be a potential hazard point for him. After working out, he tends to seek out flirtatious conversations with women at the gym. This in turn fuels his lust for pornography and masturbation.
- Caitlyn realizes that her hours spent scrolling through TikTok and Instagram feeds create an emotional disconnect from real relationships. Over the past few months, she has slowly retreated from friends at church, and now she spends a large part of her time on sexually explicit websites to fill the void.

Evaluating how believers steward their time allows patterns to be spotted early. You can help them to develop a better life structure by

- looking at samples of how they spend their time. Get them to write out their schedules or talk through them with you.
- identifying areas in their lives where there are potential problems. Work together to discover where sin typically shows up, where bad habits develop, where they run into harmful triggers, where their lives are unfruitful, where there is no rest or worship.
- developing and inserting healthy and spiritually enriching new patterns, rather than just getting rid of bad structural patterns.
- making suggestions for where and how things can change. Uncover opportunities for change by asking questions like
  o When are you having time in the Word and prayer?
  o Do you spend enough time with other believers? Is your fellowship with other believers encouraging or superficial?
  o Are you going to church? What is that time like? If your time in church is not edifying, what needs to change?
  o Are you sleeping properly, eating healthily, and getting exercise?
  o Where is rest built into your life? When do you get to slow down?
- asking them to come up with better structures for their lives and to either write them out or talk through them with you.

Hunter and Caitlyn stepped back, looked at the details of their lives, and made structural changes to help them to enjoy the good, avoid temptation, and find greater delight in God and their lives. Structure on its own doesn't sanctify them. It doesn't solve their problems. It doesn't magically make their lives better. But it can be a means God uses to provide believers with a greater opportunity—to trust God, build edifying relationships, make better decisions, and resist temptation.

After doing a life audit, Hunter realized that he should set up a meeting with a Christian brother immediately after his gym workouts. That would help him to avoid lingering in the gym and flirting with women, heading off the temptations that stirred his desire to look at porn and masturbate. Hunter said, "If I can stick relatively to my plan, it allows little to no time for me to fall."

Caitlyn added, "The more structure I have in my day, the less likely I am to be tempted to fall. I saturate my life with Scripture, so I'm constantly being reminded of truth. I set up my day so I read my Bible when I would normally be tempted. Currently, I have Ephesians 5:5 and 1 Corinthians 6:9–10 as daily reminders on my phone and have them on a sticky note on my computer."

If individuals plan wisely, they can throw up roadblocks to vulnerable moments and put themselves in a better position to fight the sin overall. When they create these structures, they should make sure that other people know about them. They should tell their closest friends and ask them to hold them accountable. If they make a plan, they need a community of friends to help them in their mission.

STRATEGY 8: WHEN YOU FAIL, RUN TO THE LORD

Solomon writes, "For the righteous falls seven times and rises again, but the wicked stumble in times of calamity" (Prov. 24:16). Both the righteous and the wicked face hard things in their lives and fall as a result, but, unlike the wicked, the righteous will rise again.

Sexual sin is a daily battle, and for some it lasts for extended seasons. A believer falls and needs to get back up many days. I (Deepak) wrote earlier about Axel, who often fell into temptation and masturbation. Too often, in the first few hours and days after he engaged in sexual sin, his heart became fertile ground for the Enemy. The devil used those times to accuse Axel and cause him to despair through his lies and deception. Satan would whisper, "You're never going to win, Axel, so give up."

One pernicious lie that Axel shared with me caused him to fear going to God to seek forgiveness. "I knew it was wrong . . . and I did it, consciously—so how do I immediately go apologize for something I did? It feels contrived sometimes because if I had *really* repented yesterday, I wouldn't be here again today." Satan had been whispering to Axel, "Surely you don't think God is going to forgive you *again*?"

and "Surely you can't come to him *again* after what you've done."
Do you see how lies like these can keep strugglers from coming to
the Lord in repentance?

Yet we know that confession and repentance before the Lord are
vital for our survival. King David certainly knew that well:

> For when I kept silent, my bones wasted away
> > through my groaning all day long.
> For day and night your hand was heavy upon me;
> > my strength was dried up as by the heat of summer.
> I acknowledged my sin to you,
> > and I did not cover my iniquity;
> I said, "I will confess my transgressions to the LORD,"
> > and you forgave the iniquity of my sin. (Ps. 32:3–5)

David's sins of adultery and murder were painful. His "bones wasted
away" through his "groaning all day long." The Lord's hand was
"heavy" on him. Yet David knew where to turn—he went to the
Lord with his sin, confessed his transgression, and sought God's forgiveness.

The forgiveness of God is the hope of Christians. It's the hope
of anyone who confesses her sexual sin. It's the light at the end of a
dark path. Though daily struggles can feel hopeless—and, at times,
pointless—we can't give up on God's forgiveness. Winston Smith
declares, "Habits die hard, especially ones that deliver the kind of
excitement and immediate rush that sexual lust does. You won't simply have to say no just once, but many times, and sometimes you will
fail. It's important for you to understand that no matter how many
times you fail and no matter how long this battle lasts, you cannot
exhaust God's love and forgiveness. . . . Take responsibility for your
sin, trusting that God will forgive and cleanse you because of his
faithfulness, not yours."[7]

Encourage your friend, no matter how hard things might be, to
trust in God's faithfulness. No matter how many times he falls, God
will be waiting to pick him up if he repents and puts his trust in him.

STRATEGY 9: DON'T FIGHT ALONE

Because sexual sin is isolating and brings condemnation, believers (unfortunately) often try to attack this problem all by themselves. It's important that they not just confess to the Lord but also find other Christians to confess to and get help from (see James 5:16). If your friend has spoken only to you, offer a challenge: ask him to open up to one or two other believers. Ask him to show humility and transparency to others. Plead with him to entrust his struggle to those whom he knows are mature and wise.

Although it's helpful for the struggler to pull a few friends into his inner circle, you should also make sure he is committed to a local church. Genuine Christian community is a real gift. In it, fellow believers commit to walk alongside the struggler for his good and for God's glory. They give the struggler a chance to see, taste, observe, and learn what living faith looks like in a fallen world. It's like watching Christianity in 3D. Make sure your friend has committed his life to a gospel-preaching, Jesus-loving local church.

STRATEGY 10: SERVE AND LOVE OTHERS

There's one last thing. Encourage your friend to serve others. As we saw in the last chapter, masturbation is the antithesis of love and service. It's self-serving and self-focused. That's not only wrong, it's anti-Christian. Here's the basic DNA of Christianity: (1) *Because* Christ humbled himself by taking on the form of a servant and becoming obedient to the point of death on a cross (see Phil. 2:7–8), (2) we should do nothing in selfish ambition or vain conceit but in humility (like Christ) count others more significant than ourselves (see Phil. 2:3–6). Through his life and death on the cross, Christ left us an example of serving and loving others. Rather than engaging in self-indulgence, escapism, isolation, and self-focus, we are called by Jesus to this same humble life of self-sacrificial love and service for others.

Masturbation turns a believer in on himself. The gospel turns a believer outward, toward others, in faith, service, and love. Pastor and author Winston Smith tells us, "Rather than living in a world of selfish pleasures, learn the joys of being with and serving others in love. Christ's love is made complete in you as you share it with others. . . . God promises that, as you live a life of love by trusting in Christ, God's love will become visible through you. What could be more meaningful than making God's love visible to others?"[8]

Ask your friend if her masturbation habit pulls her away from others. Does it feel costly to her, or is it all about self-gratification? Does it display love, or does it downgrade it?

Masturbation is self-indulgent. Christian love and service are costly. But this cost is well worth it, because sacrifice and service become a very visible display of gospel love.

THE END OF THE MATTER IS THE GLORY OF GOD

The strategies in this chapter aren't meant to be applied apart from a loving, thriving relationship with the Lord. Too often, we find that people seek to implement a strategy here and there—in their own strength. The starting point for these strategies is our desire to bring glory to God through the way we live and breathe.

BUILD A RESCUE PLAN

Personal Reflection

You can't teach others something that you're not doing yourself. Before you work through these strategies with your friend, consider the following questions about yourself: Where do I need to grow in guarding my heart, trusting in God's forgiveness, and serving others? Am I aware of the triggers that tempt me to sin? Am I believing and trusting in Christ?

Potential Problems

Consider the ways the devil is messing up your friend. Does he isolate her? Is she ignorant of her triggers? Is she convinced that she's unworthy of God's forgiveness and love? Is she characterized more by selfishness than by self-sacrifice? Is she focused more on timelines than on her relationship with Christ?

Practical Step

Don't try to implement all ten strategies at one time. Pick one or two and work through them with your struggling friend. If you are not sure where to begin, pray and read over the strategies with your friend, then see if you can agree on a starting point together.

Prayer

Lord, help my friend not to tolerate masturbation. Rather, strengthen him to turn to Christ. Jesus is more than worthy of his utmost time, love, and affections. Make every part of his life a shining display of your truth and love. O God, help him to always glorify you. In Jesus's name, amen.

6

THE SIMILARITIES AND DIFFERENCES BETWEEN MEN AND WOMEN

*The biggest problem with using fantasy, erotica and
pornography is that they damage our relationship with God.*
—Helen Thorne, Purity Is Possible

Idolatrous and lonely, selfish hearts don't belong to one gender.
—Ellen Dykas, "Women and Sexuality: The Church's Blind Spot"

Andrea grew up in a loving home with two parents and two brothers. Her childhood was fairly happy—she made several good friends on her block, played soccer, and went to Disney World when she was eight.

Her entire life shifted in her junior year of high school. When an illicit ad popped up on her screen, she clicked. She didn't expect to be transported to a forbidden world. She saw images of men and women having sex, and she didn't have words or terms for what she was watching. Something awoke in her that was hard to put back to sleep, so Andrea went back the next day for more. Her parents never talked to her about how bodies develop and change, much less about sexual desires and sex itself. When her parents were not paying attention, Andrea jumped on an unmonitored computer and searched out more. She quickly moved from looking at pornographic images to watching videos and entering chat rooms. She was hooked, and a year later, her life was consumed by pornography.

A double life ensued. Andrea lived up to the "good girl" role she had so carefully cultivated, but she walked around with immense guilt and shame. Though she'd often tell herself, "This has got to stop," it never did. When she graduated high school close to the top of her class, she felt like a hypocrite. By her mid-twenties, her enslavement to pornography and masturbation had grown to the point that it ruled her life. Her health suffered—she lost sleep and was often stressed—as she spent hours surfing the web to get more. Andrea was in a demanding job, but she refused to let go of her pursuit of porn. She longed to break free, but she didn't know how.

Carrie's struggle is different. Over coffee one day, two of her closest friends talked about reading a popular romance novel. Each had strong opinions about the main characters. When Carrie bought a copy the next day and consumed it, she entered into a world that no one in her evangelical Christian upbringing had ever talked about. A war erupted in her heart. She knew that reading a steamy, sexually explicit story was wrong, yet it thrilled her. The sexually explicit content troubled her conscience, but she rationalized it by saying to herself, "It's just words on a page, not explicit pornographic images." Sadly, it didn't take much effort for her to override her conscience and continue.

This first novel was just a start for Carrie. Her appetite grew. Over the next few years, her fascination with erotica took her through more romance books and fan fiction. She read to fill her cravings, but her yearnings were never satisfied. She always wanted more.

Carrie's mind was filled with the scenes she had read. Over time, she constructed and plunged into a dark fantasy world. When relationships were hard, the characters in her fantasy world gave her all the attention, sex, and comfort she ever wanted. In her make-believe world, no man would, or could, tell her no.

London felt embarrassed when she confessed to her boyfriend, Derek, that she struggled with porn and fantasy. She was convinced he would break up with her because women aren't supposed to struggle with this kind of thing. He'd think she was a freak. But Derek didn't break it off. He forgave her and expressed his love for her. She was shocked. She'd spent so many years mired in shame that she didn't know what to do with his gracious response.

Derek and London eventually married, yet London's struggles continued. She had a hard time telling any of her girlfriends, because she knew they would think poorly of her. But Derek was a good source of accountability. She would fall and hide from him, and he would figure it out. Derek had struggled with pornography when he was younger and found victory over his porn addiction several years ago. She yearned for the same freedom.

Because both men and women struggle with sexual sin, in this book we've carefully offered examples of both men and women who struggle with porn and masturbation. For years, people have emphasized porn and masturbation as a man's problem and haven't thought about how women commit sexual sin or may be victims of it. In fact, women bear an added burden because they tend to be treated as sexual objects rather than people to be valued and treasured.

Our culture is filled with many lies and myths about what women feel, think, and experience when it comes to sex. To thoughtfully consider the problem of porn, we've got to talk about how women are affected, dispel the lies and myths about women and sexual sin, and speak truth into this whole issue.

The overall aim of this chapter is to share similarities and differences between the genders when it comes to sexual sin. How do we best describe men's and women's feelings, thoughts, and experiences related to this topic? We don't want to be simplistic in our approach. Yet, by distinguishing the genders, we'll make some generalities.

These are broad brush strokes. There is always variation when we talk about *specific* people in *specific* situations. This chapter is not an attempt to fit everyone into a one-size-fits-all paradigm, but many should be able to relate to what it says.

HOW DO WOMEN VIEW SEX?

We can better understand how women view sex using five *P*s: personal relationships, possession, power, pairing, and parenting.[1]

Personal Relationships

For many women, sex is about personal relationships. Genuine, heartfelt sex that's tender and loving is found in the midst of honesty, trust, safety, and security in a relationship. A woman's view of sex often goes beyond a physical act or a lust-filled experience. It's about a healthy, loving, emotionally intimate relationship between two people who trust each other and are committed to one another. Such a view of sexuality is on target with how God designed it.

Many women have a robust view of sex and desire it more than they would be willing to admit. Yet an honest mutuality in sex, a loving give-and-take in intimacy, is so rarely found. Our culture has ruined our disposition toward sexuality—it twists, distorts, and exploits it. That's the backdrop. Standing on center stage are the men who make sex a difficult experience for many women. Sadly, men often hurt women and taint sex.

For many women, personal relationships matter more than the sex itself. A girlfriend feels insecure about herself, and she knows that sexual favors will keep a man interested in her (at least for a while). Her focus is on the boyfriend, not the sex. She desires for him to pay attention to her. She desires to be desired.

The fact that women are very keen on relationships is no surprise. The porn industry gets this. Porn used to be made by men for men. A new trend started when women got behind the camera. Women made femme porn—a brand geared explicitly for women. Reporter Cereb Gregorio observes that in femme porn "women are depicted as objects of desire rather than merely a means for a guy to get off. They are slowly seduced and romanced into having sex with sincerity and smart conversation."[2]

Possession

Most people think of sex as something that's given to men for them to celebrate and, in Christians circles, be discipled in. Women view sex as something that is not theirs to enjoy or possess. It is something that men have been given rather than them. Think in terms of *Playboy*, the *Sports Illustrated* swimsuit issue, advertisements,

Hollywood movies, and modern-day soap operas and television series. Women are sexually exploited and show up in skimpy outfits, while the men walk around fully dressed. Sex is regarded as a man's gift to delight in.

A woman with a strong sex drive is viewed differently than a man in similar situations. Men see having sex as a right; women are seen as needing to serve men in this area. Many women have internalized this view. Wives tend to think of having sex as their duty rather than their delight; unfortunately, this is what many have been taught.

Power

The sexual exploitation, abuse, and objectification that women undergo create a power dynamic that can ruin their sexual experience. Because abuse and harassment are far too common, many women see sex as disgusting and scary. Because they have been treated in demeaning ways—harassed, hurt, belittled, whistled at—sexuality as a whole is tainted. The poor treatment of women leads to a huge disconnect in their understanding of how sex can be a part of God's good design.

There is another aspect to the power component for women. A power shift is taking place in our culture. Historically, women have been oppressed and repressed—that's obviously not right. The reaction has been a push toward women's liberation—women's freedom to express themselves and recover power. Rather than be passive partners, women want to be domineering. Rather than being seen as part of a man, a woman has a right unto herself.

In a world where a woman can feel dominated or overrun by misogynistic men, sex can become a place where women can feel power over men. A woman knows that her sexual appeal can manipulate a man into doing what she wants; she can control a man even in the kind of sexually explicit acts that occur in the bedroom, where she gets to dominate.

Pairing

For many women, sex is about pairing. Sex is a way for a woman to get a boyfriend or a husband. She sees sex as a necessary means of getting what she truly wants in a relationship—acceptance, attention, affirmation.

Pornography can seem like a safe refuge and haven for women who struggle with singleness and loneliness. Online pornography functions as a stand-in relationship that is available and convenient.

Parenting

A lot of women want to have children and the joy of expressing maternal love. Thus, some view sex primarily in regard to its biological functioning. It's a means to get children. Once childbearing is done, the role of sex is done. However, childbearing is not usually the man's goal. Not surprisingly, for women in their forties, sex in marriage is different.

THE TRUTH ABOUT WOMEN AND SEXUAL SIN

In Christian circles, and in parts of the wider culture as well, an all-too-common assumption is that porn, lust, masturbation, and fantasy are only a man's problems. The thinking goes like this: Men are visual; women are relational. Men lust and crave sex; women don't. Porn is about visual things—viewing images and videos—so this must be a man's dilemma, not a woman's. Women are essentially asexual.

Let's test these assumptions to see whether they're fact or folklore.

Women Look at Hard-Core Pornography

Long gone are the days when a woman was expected to stay at home and a man would go to the strip club or walk away from a newspaper stand with a sultry magazine in a brown paper bag. The Internet has leveled the playing field so women now have easy, equal, and free access to porn. Open access to the Internet makes it possible for a woman to view as much porn as she wants in the privacy of her own home.

Pornhub is one of the top-ranking porn sights in the world with 42 billion visits in 2019 and 115 million visits per day. In its 2019 annual review, it reported that women viewers made up a minimum of 10 percent of all hits worldwide. In several places in the world (Paraguay, Ecuador, Namibia, and several countries in Central America), women made up as much as 50 percent of the viewers. The worldwide average for women viewers on Pornhub was 32 percent.[3]

In our research, we've learned three things:

1. According to Covenant Eyes, about 20 to 35 percent of women are intentionally accessing porn.[4]
2. There is a generational gap among women. The Internet became common in the mid-1990s, and the iPhone showed up in 2007. Generation Z women (those born in 1997 or after) are the most affected generation. Millennial women use porn less frequently, especially older millennials.[5]
3. Sexual addiction among women is a *growing* and *significant* problem.

Because of the way shame affects women (which we'll see shortly), the actual numbers are probably higher. With the Internet and Internet-capable technology so readily available, porn use is prevalent and accepted among today's teen girls and college-aged women. Author, blogger, and former porn addict Jessica Harris says, "The attitude among Christian girls in Generation Z . . . is very much 'what's the big deal? *Every girl watches pornography.*' I heard that from a twelve-year-old girl in a church where I spoke. Some youth groups have reached out because anonymous surveys of their youth groups showed 100% of the girls struggled with pornography. And they had no idea it was that bad."[6]

Survey data about porn use among women is vastly understudied.[7] It is hard to find detailed studies that show what's happening among elementary-school and teenage girls. Based on our counseling experience and conversations with parents, we foresee a sad reality: there is a tidal wave coming among elementary-school and teenage girls. Get yourself ready. When women in generations Z and Alpha (those born in 2010 and after) arrive in our churches as adults, a tsunami will hit our shores.

The myth is that *only men struggle with porn.* The truth is that women struggle with porn too. And the younger we go, the bigger the problem gets.

Women Can Be Visually Stimulated and Aroused by Sexual Imagery

Let's test another assumption—*only men are visually stimulated and aroused by images*—by looking at what's happening in the brain when pornography is viewed, regardless of gender. Thomas James, a neuroscientist at the University of Indiana, says, "When we put people in [the functional magnetic resonance imaging (fMRI) scanner] and show them sexual stimuli, the response in the brain is two to three times stronger than any other kind of image or stimulus I've ever used."[8] The brain responds to sexual images much more than it does to nonsexual images. It's wired to react strongly. That makes sense, since a brain's response to sexual visual stimulation is key to facilitating procreation.

Both men's and women's brains have heightened responses to sexual imagery.[9] But what (if anything) is different about a woman's brain? Notably, Kim Wallen, a researcher at Emory University, found that a man's brain had stronger activation in the hypothalamus ("the seat of base sexuality") and the emotional centers of the brain. But when Wallen surveyed women, they reported a greater overall experience of arousal compared to the men who were shown porn images.[10] The researchers were not sure why this difference occurred, but they suspected that men and women were looking at different parts of the imagery. If so, that might account for the difference.

In their follow-up study, Wallen and her team did brain scans of hundreds of men and women as they viewed photos from free porn websites. Their brains were scanned, and their eye movements were tracked. They found that women looked at the pornographic imagery just as long as men and that women found the images just as arousing as men did. There is no difference there.

To summarize, both men's and women's brains showed lots of

activation in response to pornographic images. Women were visually stimulated and aroused by images, and for the same amount of time. They just focused on different things when they looked.[11] The neurochemistry tells us that it's just not true that women don't react to pornography, nor is it true that they can't get visually stimulated and aroused by it (and also hooked on it). Turns out that the *only men are visually stimulated and aroused* assumption is folklore. Scientific research shows it's false.

Women Lust, Fantasize, and Masturbate

Both statistics and science show that women look at hard-core porn. Yet another problematic assumption in many evangelical churches is that *women don't struggle with lust, masturbation, and fantasizing.* Consequently, heterosexual women experience considerable shame connected to their lustful desires, self-stimulation, and sensual thought lives. One researcher comments, "I think heterosexual women still are influenced by the traditional conception of a proper woman being a pure woman, someone who doesn't have sex unless its purpose is to express love or to have children."[12]

A woman can feel like a lonely misfit for experiencing sexual desire. Elise sits in church on a Sunday morning. Her pastor speaks about sex and tells the men to pursue their wives, quoting Proverbs 5: "Let your fountain be blessed, and rejoice in the wife of your youth. . . . Let her breasts fill you at all times with delight; be intoxicated always in her love" (vv. 18–19). Elise thinks, "He gets to enjoy me, but what about me? What do I get to enjoy? Don't you see that I struggle with lust too?" When her pastor talks about lust, he addresses the men, not women, as if women never struggle.[13]

Elise looks around at the sea of happy faces on Sunday mornings, and she's left to think, "I'm the only one who struggles like this," or, even worse, "There must be something wrong with me." She has been addicted to porn for several years. Guilt, shame, loneliness—they've become all too common in her experience. As her addiction grows worse, she hides and isolates herself, which cuts her off from any real source of help.

Jessica Harris writes, "Both men and women have sex drives. Both men and women can be tempted visually. Both men and women lust. The difference is that we talk about these things as if all men struggle with them and no woman ever has. I can't tell you the number of e-mails I get from women who thought they were alone in their struggle. Meanwhile, when we address men, it's assumed that they've experienced this temptation. That double standard smothers women in shame. . . . [A woman] starts to fear that no man will ever want a woman like her."[14]

Fantasy is a massive issue among women. Alicia, a single Christian woman, forays into a fantasy world of her own making. She walks away from a hard job and difficult relationships into an imaginary land where she's liked by everyone and desired by attractive men, where she can get as much sex as she wants and there is no one to question her. In a lonely life, her fantasizing makes her temporarily feel alive. Helen Thorne writes, "Who doesn't want to be part of a scenario where our wildest dreams come true, in a fantasy where we are in charge and everyone around us is pandering to our every desire? There are no limits to who we can be, what we can try or who else can be there. We're surrounded by other people, but immune from getting hurt (unless, of course, that is what we are seeking). In fantasy-land, no one says no to us; everyone is keen to jump to our agenda; and that feels wonderful."[15]

This temporary world is hollow to the core. It presents an alternate refuge to turning to the Lord. The same carnal lusts and idols that perpetuate porn addictions also create a predilection for fantasy. And the self-justifications can keep a woman stuck in her sin: "It's only in my head, so no one is getting hurt." "God's forgotten me, so I deserve something for my troubles." "When God gives me a man, I'll stop." As we've seen in part 1, Jesus tells us that it's not just physical adultery that's a problem—lustful thoughts are also a sin (see Matt. 5:27–30).

Does a fantasy life have any consequences? Sure it does. Thorne articulates the futility of this venture: "In a few short seconds, you go from being in the arms of your ideal partner to sitting in solitary confinement. You come down to reality with a thud. And that makes everything worse. The lonely feel lonelier, the ugly feel uglier, the unfulfilled feel tossed aside, the curious are no closer to their dreams and the abused become weaker still. The fleeting fancy that offered so much disappears in a moment and leaves us utterly isolated."[16] The letdown leads women to get further addicted to their own fantasies.

If fantasy is a major issue, masturbation too is a common struggle. A woman may use masturbation to finish off a fantasy or as a self-soother when she's lonely. Although she may cut off access to pornography or throw her erotic literature in the trash bin, giving up masturbation is not so simple. She's fighting both the addictive nature of the release as well as its self-comfort/self-soothing aspect.[17] They are both difficult to overcome.

AN IMPORTANT TRUTH ABOUT MEN AND SEXUAL SIN

Howard recently approached me (Deepak) to help him to sort out his struggles with pornography. He knew how much his porn addiction was hurting his marriage, and he desperately wanted it to end. As I pressed into his life, Howard realized that he looked at porn for a sense of affirmation and approval. He rarely received encouragement from his wife. There was constant tension and arguing at home. He ran to porn because he felt so discouraged in his marriage. Prior to our conversations, Howard knew it was wrong to look at porn; he'd just never realized *why* he did it.

Although there are dozens of myths related to men and sexual sin, we'll examine just one: *men pursue porn only because of lust.* Men are stereotyped as sex-crazed creatures who have no depth to their lives. Pick any leading role in a Hollywood rom-com—you'll find men pursuing romance and sex, but these men have very little substance. There are men who live for more than just sex. Men have hearts, from which emerge their genuine hopes, dreams, goals, and motivations. One of the many reasons men pursue porn is for a sense of comfort, validation, emotional connection, and affirmation. It's not just women who long for deeper connections in relationships; men do too.

DIFFERENCES BETWEEN MEN AND WOMEN

While we've noticed many similarities between men's and women's battles with sexual sin, there are also differences in the areas of motivations, shame, erotica, and masturbation. A wise helper will ask good questions and provide a safe environment for the struggler to share and be transparent. Don't make assumptions, but seek to understand and know the person in front of you.

Motivations

Where there is porn, there are deeper heart issues that drive the sexual addiction. A person's heart is overrun with deeper motivations (the internal heart issues) that stand behind his or her sexual acts (the behavior). Single men and women may feel a sense of *entitlement* to a spouse or a chance at sex, even when God has denied this to them, or *insecurity about their body image*, which drives them to look for ideal body types while searching through porn images. Nevertheless, men and women may have very different reasons for acting out.

On a surface level, when a man watches porn, he experiences lust. As he looks at a woman's body on a screen, he feels a greedy craving for the visual stimulation of a woman's nudity (and/or her sexual acts) and the arousal that comes with it. This is much more than an appreciation of her physical beauty. He experiences carnal lust for her body. His own body awakens in response, and he's drawn into the desires of his flesh. On a deeper level, the man's internal war may be defined by such things as a pursuit of adventure in a relatively boring life (also known as the Indiana Jones syndrome) or a sense of affirmation, validation, or comfort.

On a surface level, women too may pursue sex for physical pleasure and for the satisfaction of physical intimacy and touch. But on a deeper level, for many women sex is not about sex. It's not the ultimate end of a woman's pursuit. Though a woman may experience desires for physical pleasure or to be visually stimulated, that's not what is foremost for her. Sex isn't about the greedy, lustful pursuit of a man's body, though there can be great satisfaction from physical touch and intimacy. The deeper issues (to offer a sampling, not an exhaustive list) may be tied to emotional connection in relationships, control, and also stress relief.

Shame

Shame is common for those with addictions. It's as normal as water in an ocean. Shame and addiction are virtually inseparable.

Men and women both struggle with shame, but there's a major difference: women live with much *more* shame than men. After surveying 3,600 men and women, therapist and pastor Jay Stringer discovered that for both men and women "shame was the biggest predictor of pornography use," but the women he surveyed "experienced shame at nearly double the rate of men."[18] Women experience a double dose of shame. Why? Consider three factors that add up to a deafening silence that compounds a woman's shame.

Parents don't converse with their kids about sex.[19] Sure, a parent may zoom in during the teenage years to have "a talk"—but the approach is to get in and out as fast as possible, because the topic of sex is embarrassing and awkward. Teenagers and younger children are left to figure things out on their own and are educated about sex more by peers, schools, movies, and online material than by their very own parents.

The church doesn't talk about sex in helpful ways. We've already mentioned that a pastor can contribute to a woman's shame if he talks about sexual immorality as only a man's issue. Add to this the fact that a lot of churches don't talk about sex or promote a church culture in which the hurting, addicted, and ashamed can openly seek help. A church culture makes a woman's shame worse when it's more superficial than transparent, more rules-based and legalistic than grace-centered, and more performance-driven than loving. A porn struggler is more inclined to hide and put on a happy face on Sundays than to be transparent and honest with those around her. If things get bad, a woman runs to the host of professionals outside her church to seek honest, thoughtful, transparent conversations rather than pursuing any kind of genuine help within her church. Pastors must think about how to shape a church culture in which addicted women, not just men, can be helped.

Gender and generational gaps intensify a woman's shame.[20] There is no generational gap among men. From the very beginning of the sexual revolution, *Playboy* and *Hustler*, strip clubs, and the adult sections at VHS rental stores were for men. Consequently, generations of men have grown up on hard-core pornography, first in print magazines and then on the Internet. Step into the subculture of men helping men, and you'll find that men's groups and accountability among men are fairly common today. It's normal for men to seek out other men to help them in their struggles with pornography and masturbation.

It's not the same for women. Baby Boomers don't talk about pornography and masturbation; it is not typical of the post–World War II generation. On the other end of the generation gap, Gen Z women have grown up with screens, smartphones, and Internet access. They experience pornography as a normal part of life. Shows rated TV-14 depict teenagers and young women talking to each other about porn and masturbation as if it's the expected and natural thing to do. As a *porn is norm* culture takes over, it will diffuse the shame that has long been the ruling dynamic in most church cultures. What we expect is for generations Z and Alpha to be more addicted to porn and masturbation and for their perspectives to be vastly different from Baby Boomers'.

In the middle of this gap, Generation X and Millennial women talk to each other about topics like romance, sexual temptation, and coveting, but they're embarrassed to open up about pornography and masturbation. Author and counselor Hayley Satrom told us that women start counseling sessions with the line "I've never told anyone this" before opening up about their pornography and masturbation habits. Former university women's dean Jennifer Kintner told us, "I don't know if I ever had a woman bring up pornography or masturbation without me first saying the words. Some would come to discuss struggling with sin, or struggling to sleep, or hating the darkness, or needing to not be alone . . . but often by the prompting of the Spirit, I would just wonder and ask and they would feel such relief [because I brought it out into the open]. We weren't allowed to discuss these things."[21]

Because of the silence of parents, pastors, and fellow church members, women are left to self-diagnose how and why their addictions happen. As erotic literature becomes more common reading material among women, and the *porn as norm* expectation takes over, we expect to see a change among these middle generations.

Erotica

Though some men do read erotica, it's much more common among women. E-books and e-readers allow a woman to read erotica in public areas without worrying that others will notice.[22]

Although porn marketed to women was already available, erotica entered into mainstream acceptance in March 2012 when E. L. James's erotic novel *Fifty Shades of Grey* was released by a major publisher. Its plot revolves around a relationship between the sadomasochistic billionaire Christian Grey and his sexual servant, Anastasia Steele. After the book came out, millions of women, including Christians, consumed it and had no problem with it. In fact, *Fifty Shades* became the fastest selling paperback of all time, selling more than 150 million copies worldwide and being translated into roughly fifty languages.[23]

What was taboo—women reading erotic literature and talking with each other about dominant-submissive relationships—shifted into the mainstream. It became socially acceptable. Journalist Alexandra Alter boasts, "The series . . . [paved] the way for more boundary-pushing erotica, and changed the way that major retailers and entertainment companies catered to female desire. . . . James became a taboo-breaking evangelist for certain kinds of sexual fantasies that women were often silent about, or ashamed of."[24] Sales of sex toys (including bondage toys used in the book and movie) increased. Thorne suggests, "The characters are doing things that women didn't have the courage to ask their husbands to do. . . . Some women want to vicariously be living these relationships themselves."[25]

The younger stepsister of popular erotic literature is erotic fan fiction. In fan fiction, amateur authors use characters from copyrighted material, such as TV shows, movies, music, and popular books, in their stories and typically post them online anonymously for others to read free of charge. Some see fan fiction as a legitimate way to practice writing and get constructive feedback. Others think it's merely a way to express "desires that could not be articulated, much less acted out, in our real world."[26] Millions of people write fan fiction, and one popular fan fiction website reported that 75 percent of its stories are romantic or sexual in nature.[27]

Masturbation

Everyone knows that masturbation occurs. No one talks about it. In the last two chapters, we explored reasons why masturbation is wrong and strategies for fighting it. Now we'll distinguish differences between why members of both genders masturbate.

For a man, masturbation typically follows pornography use. It's the end result of his pursuit of pornography. A man uses porn (an external action) or fantasizes (an internal action) as a prompt, which provokes arousal of his body. He finishes off this experience with masturbation so that he can reach climax and orgasm. For a woman, masturbation may follow porn use, yet plenty of women masturbate for reasons other than pornography.

While it's true that masturbation follows pornography use most of the time, a man or woman may move beyond a pornography addiction and continue to struggle with masturbation. That shouldn't be a surprise since the flesh, when denied access to pornography, finds other ways to satisfy its cravings.

Men and women have many reasons for masturbation in common. They may feel a sense of entitlement—for example, they deserve it because they are still single and "should" be married. Maybe they're bored, isolated, and wallowing in self-pity. Or they're stressed and anxious, and masturbation provides immediate relief. Perhaps they've used it to help them to fall asleep because of its self-soothing qualities.

A man's and a woman's motivations for masturbating may differ, however. After a guy pursues porn, he feels so much pressure from his body's arousal and raging desires that he seeks relief from his cultivated lust. A husband might masturbate when he's not having sex in his marriage. He's convinced that he has a need that must be satisfied or that masturbation is a way to exact secret revenge on his wife.[28]

A woman may masturbate in response to her hormonal cycle, as it provides relief from pain and discomfort. Or she may do so because she's not satisfied with sex in her marriage and wants more. After intercourse, her husband feels very satisfied and falls asleep, but she stays up. On a scale of one to ten, sex with her husband was only a four. So she later engages in masturbation to get a ten. Maybe she has dreams of being adored and swooned over and intentionally engages in porn or fantasies that arouse her body. She then feels the need for a release.[29]

Regardless of the reasons, masturbation's release and pleasure, and the accompanying orgasm, can be addictive. This addictive quality, combined with a reason like the need for relief from stress or anxiety, leads men and women to essentially train their bodies to expect masturbation as a release. They may feel like they *need* it to fall asleep, just like a sleeping pill.[30]

WHAT ARE OUR TAKEAWAYS?

As we wrap up, let's consider a few implications for one-on-one discipling and for pastors and church leaders. We'll offer ways we can help and will warn against potential mistakes we can make.

Adjustments in One-on-One Discipling

Talk openly about sex. We need to get conversations about sex out into the open. Because struggling and ashamed believers are prone to hide rather than be transparent, helpers must ask. Don't assume that everything is okay.

Don't stereotype men and women. There is an abundance of myths about men and women and sex. We've got to educate ourselves on how men and women differ. When we base our help on stereotypes and assumptions about gender and sex, we run into trouble. In order to provide earnest help, we must slow down, listen to the struggling believer, not rush to assumptions, and ask questions to draw him or her out. When we give in to the myths, we hurt our counsel, blunt the effectiveness of our ministry, and make problems worse. What we have written in this chapter can serve as a broad framework for understanding the issue, but it is no substitute for compassionate, thoughtful questions asked by a wise discipler, pastor, or friend.

When a husband expresses a desire for validation or emotional connection with his wife, we've got to make a connection to his dysfunctional sexual habits. Or if a woman confesses to struggling with porn, lust, fantasy, or masturbation, we can't dismiss her troubles as nonsense and tell her what we think before we've truly listened. Harris reminds us, "Redefining her struggle before you've even listened to it could cause her to shut down and feel unheard."[31]

Recognize and adjust for the differences between men and women. A woman's approach to sex is so very different from a man's. When we acknowledge these differences, it changes how we counsel and help. For example, don't take a shortcut by handing a woman a book about a man's porn addiction.[32] Instead, find ways to speak to specific struggles—like femme porn, fantasy, and erotica—without throwing a woman into the same bucket as a man.

We don't have to throw out books for men, but let's recognize that there is a lack of resources written specifically for addicted women. "Some ministries tried to fix this," Jessica Harris reports. "One of the earliest attempts I can recall was a ministry taking their book for men and simply going through and changing the pronouns, adding a chapter on romance, and putting pretty flowers on the cover. Taking a resource written for men and coloring it pink does not make it a resource for women."[33] We can and must do better. One way is simply to be vocal about the need for evangelical publishers to provide resources for women who struggle with sexual sin.

Disciplers must take initiative, and strugglers must come out of hiding. Baby Boomer women, who are the Titus 2 older generation of disciplers, have got to go against the tendency of their generation not to talk about porn or masturbation. Instead, they must speak up. Otherwise, they leave the younger generations to figure out this problem on their own. Boomers must treat these problems seriously, show that they understand the need for help, and then set out to rescue the younger generation. The reverse is also true. The younger generations, especially Gen Z and Alpha, need to reach out to older generations. They can't spend their time conversing only with one another. They can't use the excuse that older folks are busy and they don't want to be a burden on them.

Those who are discipling women should be careful what questions they ask. Harris recalls conversations in which she shared her testimony and women reacted by saying, "Who would do such a thing?" *Who* implies that there is a certain type of woman who does this and reveals the speaker's fear that she may personally know this person. Another question to avoid is "Why would a woman do this?" *Why* questions perpetuate shame and guilt. They imply that there is something wrong with a woman who stoops so low as to look at porn; she must be some kind of freak because she struggles with lust. Instead of *who* or *why*, we need to ask *how* questions: How can I help? How can we change our church culture? How do I need to change to become a better helper?[34]

The fact that women experience a double dose of shame changes our approach. Because women feel so much shame over their porn use, we make concerted efforts to address a woman's shame. The combination of self-condemnation and condemnation from others, parental silence regarding sex, and careless comments at the church shape a woman's shame and complicate this issue. How many evangelical approaches to porn problems center on the sin of lust rather than the cycles of guilt and shame that bog down a woman? Once a woman is addicted, she feels trapped and depressed. She self-condemns, and her faulty coping strategies lead her deeper into a pit. *She feels like God is sick of her.* Harris explains:

> I [could] share with you email after email of Christian women who are absolutely convinced that God is disgusted with them and doesn't want anything to do with them. The shame is so deep and so dark that it is driving them from the very One who can set them free. Until they can grasp that God is for them, that He desires their freedom, and that He welcomes them to actually find refuge in him, they aren't going to believe that is an option. They go drink from broken cisterns because they're convinced there's a flaming sword on the path to Living water.[35]

We've got to do more to help address this overwhelming shame. Far too many are entangled and left on their own to sort this out.

Don't treat erotica or fan fiction as insignificant. As we noted above, some women don't enter the forbidden through porn but through more socially acceptable sexually explicit romance novels or a zillion free online sensual fan fiction spin-offs. Users may have a false notion that because erotica involves only words, not images, there is no relational harm or addictive quality to it, but that's not true.[36] *Fifty Shades* provoked a rise in sales of sex toys, even in brand name stores like Target.[37] *Fifty Shades* sparked imitative behaviors. We've heard or counseled women who speak of the effects of erotic literature on their souls and how hard it is to let go of it. They speak in addictive terms ("I crave it" or "I can't give it up"), take on addictive behaviors (lying, hiding, feeling guilt and shame), and talk about how hard it is to stop.

Adjustments for Pastors and Church Leaders

If you are a pastor or church leader and are reading this book to better equip yourself, thank you for taking the time to humbly read and learn! This is a good start. Nevertheless, it is just an initial step. Pastors are the primary culture shapers in their congregation. They teach the values they want the congregation to understand and hold to. They communicate these values through their teaching, leadership, and example. Here are some challenges for where to go next.

Be sensitive to women's struggle with sexual sin. A pastor's language from the pulpit needs to move from "Men, when you struggle with porn . . ." to "Men and women . . ." Presume that women *do* struggle because that's the reality, even if you've never been told until now.

Build a church culture that breaks the silence on sexual sin. Work toward a church culture in which people live in the light of God's grace. Encourage your members to be honest with each other about their sin—including porn struggles and any other variation of sexual sin.

Cultivate a church culture where it's okay to ask hard and awkward questions. If the members are invested in each other, encourage them to press into each other's sin. To root out sexual sin, you've got to ask difficult and uncomfortable questions. *When was the last time you looked at pornography? Did you masturbate? What were you looking at? Did you fantasize this past week? Are you lying to me?*

Small talk is fine. It's a normal part of most relationships. But you can't reside in comfortable small talk and, at the same time, root out the ugliness of sexual sin. Encourage your members to dig for ungodly motivations that reside in the recesses of an addict's heart but also to be gracious when they ask hard things. They should never go on a witch hunt for sin. Paul exhorts us to speak truth *in love* (see Eph. 4:15). Some of your members are good at speaking truth and pressing on hard things, but they don't show any mercy. Others are gracious and kind but don't know how to say hard things to addicts. We need *both* truth and love if we're going to lift an addict out of the bottomless pit.[38]

119

Start building a more transparent and grace-filled church culture in which addicts have the freedom to come forward and find hope. The gospel communicates love for the hurting and ashamed, but it also beckons them to come out of hiding. What changes can you make in your church, in your attitude, in how you teach and pray?

How do you create a more welcoming church for men and women who struggle with sexual sin? Speak honestly and openly about these struggles (both in private and in your public services), give out resources that encourage men and women in their fight against lust and porn, and pray.

If I (Deepak) were the senior pastor, I'd buy copies of Helen Thorne's book *Purity Is Possible* and give it out to the congregation.

Preach about the beauty of a biblical view of sex. Porn addicts have a distorted view of true beauty and sexuality. Sex is tainted by guilt, shame, and all sorts of sin. It is shrunk down and reduced to self-fulfillment. It's dirty and idolatrous. *But God is much bigger than our sexual folly.* A Christian view of sex should be a shame-free, guilt-free, servant-hearted love for a spouse. It's about God's honor and glory, not about us. It's God's enjoyable and precious gift to a marriage, not a cheap trick to satisfy our urges. Sex is so much more, so much richer, so much more beautiful than what the world holds out to us.

CHRIST'S LOVE FOR LONDON AND LONDON'S LOVE FOR HIM

Let's go back to Derek and London, whom we met at the start of this chapter. If you look at Derek and London's lives, you'll see similarities and differences in their battles with sexual sin. They both struggled with porn, lust, masturbation, and fantasizing. Yet London's struggles with shame were twice as great as Derek's, and her reason for looking at porn and masturbating were different. When London met and dated Derek, she was still struggling, whereas he had found victory. That, too, made them different, and it only added to her confusion and shame. ("How come I can't find victory? Why did the Lord free him and not me?")

Yet here's one thing they both have in common: they love Christ. Derek's love for Christ propelled him to be servant-hearted, patient, and forgiving with London. She was astounded because she hadn't ever expected that kind of grace to be directed at her. However, what was even more amazing was Jesus. It was Christ's tender care for the Samaritan woman in John 4 that set London on a path to finally defeating sexual sin. Christ's honesty about London's past and his unbounding love amazed her. It put in her the thought "If you can love a shameful woman like her, you can also love me." She still experienced good days and bad days, but with the support of her husband, her own earnestness in fighting against sexual sin, her recommitment to church and friendships, and her growing love for the Word, London's life started to change.

We need to keep in mind the similarities and differences between men and women as we figure out how to minister effectively to strugglers. But we want to keep the chief similarity at the forefront of our work—Christ's love for us, and our love in return, can change these sexual sin struggles for the good.

BUILD A RESCUE PLAN

Personal Reflection

Where have you bought into myths and lies about women and sex? In what ways do you need to revise your views on a woman's sexuality?

Potential Problems

The shameful are reluctant to come out of hiding. The devil doesn't want them to be humble and seek help.

Practical Step

Encourage others to be honest about their sin and to not hide behind their shame. If you are a pastor, teach this value to your congregation. If you are a discipler or small group leader, encourage those within your sphere of influence. Be committed to breaking the silence, speaking up about sexual sin, and inviting the ashamed to seek help.

Prayer

Lord, I don't want to buy into the culture's myths and lies about women in particular. Help me to think biblically and graciously. Help me to be honest and to encourage others to be honest about their sin. Help us together to turn to Christ and find our refuge in him. In Jesus's name, amen!

PART 3

RESCUE THE PRISONER

By 7:15 p.m., in the dark of night, Robert Prince's C Company Rangers had crawled to a position about two hundred yards from the padlocked front gate of the prison camp. They hid close to the guard towers and patiently waited for the signal from Lieutenant John Murphy from F Company.[1] The rescue would begin at the sound of Murphy's rifle fire. He led about thirty Rangers beneath the guard tower on the northeast side of the camp.

As soon as Prince and the C Company heard Murphy's shots at 7:45 p.m., they let loose with pinpoint precision, taking out the guards in the towers and pillboxes within fifteen seconds.

In the midst of the gunfire, C Company Ranger Teddy Richardson jumped up from a ditch. After an attempt to take off the padlock with the butt of his tommy gun and a brief gunfire exchange with an enemy soldier, Richardson used his automatic pistol to break through the lock with a single shot. As he flung the lock aside and opened up the front gate, the Rangers poured in.[2]

The goal was to first neutralize the enemy officers, trucks, and tanks. The first Ranger through the gate after Richardson was a guy from Minnesota named Leland Provencher. Provencher and several other Rangers took out the officer quarters with several minutes of heavy rifle fire. A bazooka team lead by a staff sergeant from Texas named Manton Steward ran down the main road until it came to a halt directly across from the sheds that stored the enemy's trucks and armored vehicles. Steward and his team used several three-and-a-half-pound rockets to obliterate the sheds and their contents.[3]

A group of Rangers used wire cutters to cut through the barriers on the prisoners' side of the compound. Ranger Lester Malone ran up to the gate and fired his M-1 at the lock. Pulling off the lock, he opened up the gate to the prison. "We're Yanks!" he yelled. "This is a prison break! Head for the main gate!"[4]

Many books on pornography are filled with biblical principles and compelling stories. That's all well and good. But what happens when you run into the difficulties and challenges of real life? What does it look like to persevere on hard days? What happens when the flesh or the devil screams in a struggler's ear, "Live for yourself! Forget God. Why bother with him?" What does faith look like in the middle of the mess?

We've seen what we're up against, and we've seen the terrain on which we're fighting. Now we'll take things a step further. We'll move from the classroom to the bedroom, from education to application. We'll descend into the trenches to develop our practical theology—how the Bible comes to life in specific seasons, with specific people, and with specific problems.

We'll explore how disciplers of pornography strugglers can come alongside singles (chapter 7), dating couples (chapter 8), married folks (chapter 9), and children or teens with their parents (chapter 10).

Buckle up. That's where we're headed next.

7

SINGLENESS: THE PLIGHT AND POSSIBILITIES FOR SINGLES

The Son of God came into the world to save sinners. You do not need to fear telling the truth about yourself. He already knows.
—*David Powlison,* Making All Things New

Many Christians locked in a fight against pornography judge the closeness of their relationship with Christ by whether or not they've looked at porn recently.
—*Heath Lambert,* Finally Free

Carson sits in his office, flustered and frustrated with himself. "I'm never going to get over this problem." Porn has been an integral part of his life since he was twelve, when his best friend showed him lewd pictures on his smartphone. When is this going to end? Is he going to be stuck with a porn struggle for the rest of his life? Why can't he kick the habit?

Carson often lives under unrealistic stress for thirty straight days: urgent deadlines, infighting among his team members, and unrelenting pressure. He works seventy-five to eighty hours a week. His life is all about his job. This is typical of consultants in his big-name agency, which is why the burnout rate is so ridiculously high.

At the end of a thirty-day period, Carson's team usually makes its deadline with minutes to spare. He then has one or two days to lay low before the pressure starts all over again. In that brief window, he gives himself relief. Sometimes he turns to comfort food—eating far too much. More often, he indulges in mind-numbing porn as a stress reliever. He feels like he deserves some pleasure—he is entitled to it after weeks of relentless, over-the-top stress. Porn is a reward for surviving another month and putting up with a jerk of a boss. He's given up on ever defeating porn. It has become an all too familiar and friendly housemate.

Eva sits in her bedroom, seventy pages into a sexually explicit romance novel. She heard about the novel from a friend and at first thought, "I'm not going to read it." But she couldn't resist. She's spent much of her downtime in the last few years reading graphic romance books. She never takes them out of her apartment so no one else knows.

For a few years now, she's struggled with masturbation. She often feels guilty about her pattern: she indulges in fantasy—a comforting storyline in which she meets a man, falls deeply in love with him, and gives herself to him in passion and lust—then often finishes off her fantasy with masturbation.

No one in her church ever talks about sex, and if they do, it's always mentioned as a man's problem. Eva feels ashamed and alone in her struggle. She has tried to talk to a few girlfriends. Some looked aghast that she would read sexually explicit books and masturbate, while others acted as though what she was doing was perfectly normal. She just doesn't feel right about it, though she doesn't know what to do.

Susan's boyfriend Donavan introduced her to porn. He showed her pictures and videos of things he wanted to do together. Initially, she complied by watching with him. After they had been together for several months, he got bored with her, dumped her, and moved on.

In the initial days after the breakup, Susan wallowed in self-pity. Lonely, she longed for some kind of emotional connection. She didn't understand why she turned back to the porn websites on a daily basis. In little time, the habit grew.

Susan is ashamed. She doesn't bring up the porn with her parents or her mentor at church. She can't bear the thought of how disappointed they all will be with her. She's played the part of the good

Christian girl, making it to youth group and church—all the while running around behind her parents' backs.

Porn is a common problem, yet it's not an insurmountable problem. Our goal in this chapter is to think about how single men and women can engage in the fight. We'll start with what's common in the battle for everyone, then lay out what's distinctive for singles.

HOW DO STRUGGLING INDIVIDUALS FIGHT PORNOGRAPHY?

In this section, we'll articulate what every porn struggler has to keep in mind—regardless of whether they are single, dating, or married—and then distinguish in the next section what's unique for singles. You can read about these areas in much greater detail in our companion book, *Rescue Skills*.

Here's the headline to remember: *though this sin is bad, Christ is better*. A struggling believer must do the hard work of fighting sin, shame, and the ugliness of an addiction, but the turn will ultimately come as she orients her life around the grace and love of Christ. No amount of self-effort, self-confidence, or self-discipline is the be-all and end-all to solve this problem.

Encourage Honesty and Humility

In the initial stages of helping a struggler, we've got to assess how much he wants to deal with his addiction. Carson knows he's got a problem. But even if he overcomes his shame enough to seek out help, we may find that he's not ready to listen to and accept counsel. Maybe he's prideful ("I can deal with this on my own"). Maybe he's so self-condemning that he considers himself a lost cause. Maybe he feels like God and his friends have abandoned him. In all likelihood, the complicated web of shame, sinful motivations, and self-condemnation makes it uncertain that he is prepared to fight his problem. As a discipler, make it your goal to encourage honesty and humility in strugglers. If Carson comes to a place where he's humble enough to ask for help, and he's willing to be honest about his struggles (see Prov. 24:26), then we can begin to mount a battle plan to fight against his temptations.

Shut Down Access Points

If Susan looked at porn the previous night, you know she has an open access point somewhere in her life. So pursue it. Ask her about her access points. Don't assume she knows what to do about open access. She doesn't. In fact, if she knew what to do, she wouldn't be talking with you. She's ashamed of her porn habit. She tolerates it and justifies it. Pull out her phone, open the restrictions, and talk through how to shut down access. Be sure to ask about *all* her devices (phone, laptop, tablets, e-readers, and so on).

Starve the Struggler's Selfish, Carnal Desires

Desires and cravings can overrun Carson, Eva, and Susan's lives, as is often the case with porn strugglers. A normal, healthy desire for sex can turn into a ruling desire. Why do we shut down access points? So we can starve the desires of the flesh and make no provision for it (see Rom. 13:14).

Teach the Struggler to Pursue Holy Delights

Carnal desires lead to experiences that are superficial and fleeting. More holy delights—enjoying sex within a committed marriage; relishing good food and music; laughing out loud with friends; engaging in an intimate conversation with a beloved family member or friend; accomplishing a hard task; experiencing a growing sense of who God is, what his Word says, and what he wants of you; singing the last verse of a hymn with a joyful congregation—are enduring and much more satisfying. A believer finds success when he not only says no to ungodly desires but reorients his life around more holy ones.

Pursue the Deeper Motivational Issues That Reside in the Struggler's Heart

Shutting down access points is an important first step, but behavior modification is insufficient on its own. The Bible tells us that our hearts are the command centers of our lives (see Matt. 12:33–37; Luke 6:43–45). It's out of the overflow of your heart that you think, feel, act, and live your life. Once we've constructed a firewall between Carson, Eva, and Susan and their access to porn, we explore the deeper motivational issues. Does Eva read erotica and look at porn because she's escaping the stress in her life? Does Carson feel trapped in his high-pressure job? Is he looking for freedom? Does Susan miss the months of sex with her ex-boyfriend? Is she desperately looking to find some kind of emotional connection? What other motivations stand behind their actions?

Keep in mind that many men and women lack self-awareness. They're ignorant of their heart motivations. You may be the first person to force them to slow down and take a look at their deeper motivational issues.

Take a Holistic Approach to Identity, Not a Myopic View of the Sin

If we spend all our energy fighting pornography use, we won't get very far. We can get so caught up in fighting porn that we lose sight of the bigger picture. What else matters to Susan? What other things are going on in her life? Don't reduce a believer to nothing more than a porn addict. If, in fact, Susan *is* a believer, she's so much more than an addict. She's chosen (see Eph. 1:4–5), justified (see Rom. 3:21–26), adopted (see Gal. 4:5–6), and beloved (see 1 John 3:1–3) by the King of the universe. If that's how God sees Susan, so should you.

Help the Struggler Not to Hide

The basic instinct of every embarrassed struggler is to run. That's what Adam and Eve did in Genesis 3 when God showed up. The first time I (Deepak) talked to Carson, he admitted, "I want to get up and run from this conversation, but I know I shouldn't." Do you hear that? That's shame screaming in Carson's ears: "Don't you feel dirty? Don't you feel exposed? You messed up again. Don't let him see your foolishness." Shame is a significant obstacle to getting help. It can perpetuate Carson's pornography habits by causing him to withdraw. Our initial goal is to help Carson to break his silence and come out of the darkness.

Recalibrate the Struggler's Conscience

Consistent porn use can deaden a conscience. Carson says, "I feel dead on the inside." Susan comments, "I feel numb." The Lord must quicken the conscience and bring it back to life. Our goal is to help Carson and Susan to pursue genuine repentance, faith, and obedience and, with that, to recalibrate their consciences.

Discern Fake Repentance and Encourage Genuine Repentance

If Carson feels bad about what he's done, and not much more, then he hasn't repented. You know that his repentance is *shallow* when he keeps falling back into his sin with little or no success in defeating it. Godly sorrow is good sorrow; worldly sorrow is death (see 2 Cor. 7:9–11). Point Carson to the Lord, and plead with him to run to God and beg for mercy (see Ps. 51:3–4).

Confession alone is not repentance. Many people think that if they confess to another Christian, they've repented. Not true! Confession is only the *start* of dealing with sexual sin. Verbal confession is nothing if it is not paired with godly grief and reconciliation with God. Our sin is first an offense against God.

Cultivate Faith

Faith is the wind in a struggler's sails. The best repentance is a faith-driven repentance. When Eva's focus is on Christ, she can't help but be disgusted with her sin. She must run to Christ as her only hope. Talk about Jesus again, and again, and again, until she falls in love once more with her Savior.

Pay Attention to What's Going On in Other Theaters

David Powlison describes sexual sin as a marquee, red-letter sin. It tends to grab the headlines—and our attention. Imagine Carson's life as a multiplex theater, with movies running simultaneously in different rooms.[1]

- Theater 1: his porn struggles (the main show).
- Theater 2: his stress at work.
- Theater 3: his fractured relationship with his father.
- Theater 4: his interest in a young woman at church and his confusion about whether or not he can pursue her.
- Theater 5: his anger at God for letting him repeatedly fall into sexual sin.

There's a lot going on in Carson's life. Sexual sin makes front-page news; everything else drifts into the background. Yet these different theaters are *interconnected.* If you pay attention to only the red-letter sexual sin, you do Carson a disservice. If you work at, and see progress in, other areas of his life, the sexual sin will be helped too. Don't be surprised. Whenever you throw a stone in water, there are ripples. So also in a person's heart.

Broaden the Struggler's Gaze

Pornography use may thrive in isolation, but it rarely grows alone. As disciplers, we can't let pornography problems become the main focus of our time together and ignore other theaters of life. We serve the struggler when we help her to make connections. Pastor and counselor David Dunham writes, "Porn limits the scope of a person's spiritual sight. . . . Men and women can't see their anger, their selfishness, or poor stress management. They aren't looking at the ways they generally use people, or the ways they isolate themselves, or the perfectionism they've developed. All these issues are relevant to the struggle with porn. . . . Porn is not the only area that God desires to help them grow in, and sometimes a focus on one single area [not only limits] our growth but compound[s] our obsession with that particular struggle."[2]

Carson was going through weeks of over-the-top stress, and when he got a breather, selfishness and entitlement were coconspirators

131

with the lusts of his flesh. Carson thought he deserved a little something for his efforts. As a result, he either ignored God or thought, "God, you owe this to me."

Eva struggled with the idolatry of relationships—she wanted to experience a relationship with a man. Because she hadn't been in a dating relationship for several years, she worked out her lusts by regularly fantasizing. The fantasy world became her go-to arena when her feelings of loneliness were most intense, and she hated to admit she relished it. She rarely looked at images online; rather, her lust played out in her mind.

Retool Your Accountability to Make It More Honest, Wise, and Loving

A lot of so-called accountability is useless. Susan is entrenched in porn and feels stuck. Her accountability partner, Jody, doesn't help Susan to earnestly deal with her sin and pursue faith. Unfortunately, Jody is immature and lacks solid wisdom. She is often militant and belittling, so every time Susan confesses her sin, she walks away discouraged. Jody's not consistent with Susan and not available when Susan needs to talk. Jody spends a lot of time talking about her opinions but rarely brings up God's Word.

The apostle Paul reminds us that the ultimate goal for any struggler is spiritual maturity. "Him we proclaim, warning everyone and teaching everyone with all wisdom, that we may present everyone mature in Christ. For this I toil, struggling with all his energy that he powerfully works within me" (Col. 1:28–29). Good accountability leads a struggler to greater maturity when it is brutally honest about sin; frequent enough to do good; encouraging and gracious; Word-focused, faith-filled, and prayerful; and local, not long-distance. It will also encourage the struggler to be more deeply connected to her church community, knowing that gospel communities can partner with a struggler to face her sin and pursue greater faith.

Help the Struggler to Pursue the Good and Beautiful

Pornography distorts a sense of what is good and beautiful. We reinvigorate our friends when they begin to recognize the counterfeits for what they are and acknowledge legitimate beauty—as God sees it, not as an addict sees it.

Assist the Struggler in His or Her Battle against Weariness

When Eva shows up in your office, she's exhausted. She's been battling her sexual sin for years. Not days or weeks but *years*. She's battling doubts about God's goodness and God's ability to change her. Remind Eva that her hope is not in a change of circumstances but in God himself (see Ps. 4:1, 8). Give her encouragement for the long haul.

WHAT'S DISTINCT FOR SINGLES AS THEY FIGHT AGAINST PORNOGRAPHY?

Now that we've articulated a general battle plan for fighting porn addiction, we'll distinguish the elements of the war that are unique for singles.

Certain Feelings and Desires Can Overrun Singles

Certain feelings and desires can overrun a single person's heart and life, making her shortsighted. These feelings and carnal desires can be so strong that she may struggle to envision what a porn-free life could look like.

Disciplers can help singles by drawing out their feelings and desires and examining these things in the context of honest and loving friendships and in the light of God's Word. What do we see singles struggling with as they fight? Consider the following sampling of possibilities.

Feelings of rejection. Relationships, even close relationships, can feel precarious for singles. When things don't work out, especially when it comes to dating and prospects for marriage, a single Christian feels a sense of rejection that is hard to shake. Persistent and continual feelings of rejection may become overly defining. Porn becomes a false refuge in a sea of unstable relationships.

Desires to be seen and loved. When married friends have spouses and children to occupy them, and single friends have busy social calendars or work schedules, a single man or woman may struggle with not being noticed and appreciated. He or she has a genuine desire to be seen and appreciated, and that desire is not being met.

Feelings of loneliness and self-pity and a reluctance to be vulnerable with others. In general, singles live more isolated lives than other people. Without a spouse who lives with him and intimately knows him, a single adult can hide his life without others realizing, especially if he also lives by himself and away from his parents. This isolation may foster loneliness, self-pity, and a whole host of other hard feelings.

Sexual sin makes a single's life even more isolated than the life of a married person who has the same problems. There is no parent or spouse to catch him when he looks at pornography late at night. Porn creates a felt need for so much self-protection and hiding that it's hard for the struggler to be fully transparent with others. The struggler may be willing to share some sins but not his darkest sins.

Fear regarding a lack of marriage. If marriage is held out as normal in most church cultures, then singles wrestle with thoughts like "Something is wrong with me." Singles may fear remaining virgins, never having children, or being alone in old age. Author and counselor Hayley Satrom points out, "A single woman can feel at a loss for control in moving toward marriage (particularly in a Christian environment that teaches men to initiate dating relationships). So she's not sure if she's waiting for marriage, or will never get married, and that exacerbates her struggle. Often, this leads her to blame God for not bringing her a spouse, and she can pin her sin on God since he is not answering her prayers."[3]

A sense of helplessness in dealing with their passions. If a single struggler has never experienced self-control with porn, masturbation, or sexual sin, she feels as though she's at the mercy of her flesh. When hormones rage during her menstrual cycle, a single woman may think

134

she has no reason not to give in. She doesn't know what else to do instead.[4]

A desire to be more explorative and adventurous. Singles may push boundaries with the nature and kind of porn they view. We especially see this in singles who come from sheltered backgrounds.

Can you see how all these feelings and desires can make a single's life harder? And how these feelings and desires can be coconspirators with porn struggles? Feelings say things like "You're alone in this world" or "No one knows you or sees you." Porn offers an alternative: a man or woman will never feel left out or rejected because porn is always there and consistently available. With one click on a screen, the believer can throw herself into an imaginary world of relationships and intimacy. Masturbation provides immediate payoff, and the struggler doesn't need to put in any of the work that a relationship requires: "I can feel pleasure, even if it's fleeting, without having to pursue anyone or do the hard work of persisting in my relationships."

Sin's Consequences for Others Are Less Evident during Singleness

Danny called me (Deepak) because he'd watched porn and confessed it immediately to his wife, Carla. Because this was not the first time he'd run into trouble, his sin reopened Carla's old wounds. Danny often beat himself up over how much his addiction hurt his wife.

When Danny was single, no one in his life was directly impacted by his sin.[5] As he entered into marriage and stumbled with porn, he came face-to-face with the painful reality of the cost of his sin and the consequences for his wife and children. It was something he'd never considered as a single adult.

Greg was similar to Danny. When he was single, he dabbled with porn and was blind to how it might mess things up later on. Greg met Tanisha, and they hit it off in their dating relationship. When he later confessed his struggles with porn to her, and shortly thereafter to me, I (Deepak) encouraged them to break off the relationship until he could get a handle on his porn addiction. (We'll get into my reasoning in the next chapter.) With tears in his eyes, Greg looked at Tanisha and said, "If I had only taken this seriously early on, we wouldn't be in this position right now."

Dating and marriage bring the consequences for pornography and masturbation into more acute focus because a boyfriend or a girlfriend or a spouse and children feel its painful effects.[6]

Singles Have a Particular Need for Community

In a typical church setting, singles spend time with singles, and families spend time with families. Apart from sitting next to each other in the pews on Sundays or engaging in casual talk after church, rarely do the two groups meet.

Pornography and masturbation problems feel isolating for anyone. In addition, many singles live far removed from their families and closest friends because of their work or educational training, so their loneliness is compounded. Now add one more element: singles can feel further isolated because they don't have deep relational connections in a local church community.

In teaching and counseling singles, we hold out a Titus 2 model of discipling—the spiritually mature men and women pour into the singles who struggle with pornography. We ought to instruct our congregations on the importance of community and being connected to one another—how we can break down barriers between singles and married folks, singles and seniors, singles and the children of the church.

Too many churches have a problem. Their church culture does little to nothing to help singles to meet members of other demographics in the congregation and to build deep relationships with them. How many singles feel like the only reason families reach out to them is for babysitting requests? How many singles don't reach out because they fear being a burden on busy families? How is a single person who is struggling with pornography ever going to get help with his struggles if he can't build deeper and more meaningful relational connections in his own church?

One answer is for us not just to teach the importance of discipling and community but also to live it out. Singles need to be proactive in connecting with families, and families need to incorporate singles into their lives.

Go back to Eva. What if rather than sitting at home alone every Tuesday night, fantasizing about a man, Eva is with the Browns, a solid Christian family in her church, who have an open-door policy for her to come over every week? What if the three daughters in this family—Lydia, Eden, and Noelle—develop a close connection with Eva and look up to her? What if Eva adores the daughters and looks up to Kate, their mother? What if Eva is able to have honest conversations with Kate and even Bradley, Kate's husband, after the young girls go to bed? Eva becomes so connected that she's invited over for birthday parties, and the daughters beg her to come to their soccer games. So Eva goes. Do you think Eva, after several years, will feel like a part of the Brown family? Will she feel a sense of connection with them that gives her a refuge—a safe place amidst the loneliness and storms of her life? Let's push this one step further—what if every year when the Brown family goes to the beach, Eva goes with them for the first three days? And they all love to have her there? Or when Eva goes through a season of unemployment, Bradley and Kate invite her to live with them for six months while she figures out what to do. Do you think she would say yes?

You might say to us, "You've cooked up a fantasy. Singles and families don't relate like this. This kind of dynamic just doesn't exist in churches."

We'd say in response, "This is possible because we've seen it and lived it ourselves." And we've seen it often lived out in our churches. We've experienced it and benefited personally from it (many years ago before we were both married!). And we have our own "Evas" as parts of our family lives. Singles can develop deep connections that help them to fight the battles against pornography, masturbation, idolatry, carnal desires, and the lusts that rule their lives. It is possible; it's not just a fantasy.

Some churches have a strong sense of community that is a huge ally in helping singles to fight against porn. Why is that? Because singles don't have to fight on their own. They don't have to fight the temptations of the devil in isolation. They don't have to feel alone on Saturdays when they are grocery shopping by themselves, or feel jealous when yet another couple at church announces their engagement, or feel isolated on yet another Friday night as the weekend begins. They have co-laborers—brothers and sisters and families—who stand alongside them in the war against sexual sin.

SINGLES HAVE A STRONG SENSE OF WAITING FOR GOD'S PROMISES TO BE FULFILLED

In life, we all—single and marriage alike—have to wait. You stand in a line at a fast-food restaurant that is moving more slowly than you expected. You think, "Come on! I've got things to do." Your package from Amazon is three days late, and you're frustrated because you expected it to arrive right away. When you call the doctor's office, the receptionist picks up and says, "Can you please hold?" What do you want to say? "No way! I'm really busy!" (Instead you politely say, "Uhhh . . . sure.") None of us wants to wait, yet waiting is an inevitable part of life.

God asks us to wait. God makes promises, and we as Christians have to wait on his promises to be fulfilled. God will one day return. When he returns, our salvation will be complete and we'll be like Christ. We will no longer suffer or experience sorrow or death. We'll have unhindered fellowship with Christ when we get to eternity.

We don't want to wait in general, but we also don't want to wait on God. Pornography conditions us not to wait at all. Our carnal desires are selfish, and they often demand immediate gratification. For a Christian who struggles with pornography, waiting seems especially hard.

What does this have to do with singles? While we all have to wait in life, singles in particular may feel like they have a long wait ahead of them before the promises of God are fulfilled in their lives. When they indulge in porn, they are training themselves to enjoy instant gratification for their cravings. This leads singles to be even more impatient when they don't get other things they feel entitled to, like happiness, marriage, and children.

Go back to Carson. When he hits the forty-eight-hour window of relief at the end of the month, he dives into pornography. If his business team hands in a project by 5 p.m., he's looking at porn by 6 or 7 p.m. He doesn't care about God; he doesn't care about the women he is objectifying; he doesn't care about how this habit may hurt a future wife. In Carson's little kingdom, his selfishness overrules any possibility of waiting on a future wife, fighting for purity beyond a few quickly attempted fixes, or waiting on God. He doesn't deny his lusts because his sense of entitlement tells him that he deserves to indulge himself.

There are so many lies Carson tells himself: "I'm going to end up alone." "No one can fix my problems." "God has given up on me."

His selfishness is obvious; we see it in his actions. His self-condemnation is less so because it is hidden in his quiet whispers to himself throughout many of his days. Both his selfishness and his self-condemnation can be overcome by repentance and faith. As singles starve their carnal desires and grow in their affection for Christ, they confront their entitlement and selfishness. They quiet the voices of shame and unbelief that often scream in their ears. Waiting patiently doesn't seem unreasonable anymore.

We are called, no matter the state of our hearts, no matter what season we are in, to wait on God. That means being careful to distinguish what God *has* promised singles (that our salvation will be one day complete, see Phil. 1:6) and what he *has not* promised (that we will have a spouse and children; that we'll have happiness in ways we desire).

That also means that we need to be patient as we wait on God's promises to be fulfilled. He will bring our salvation to completion. He will come back one day and take us home to be with him. We will be with him for all eternity. God is faithful. History proves that to be true. We don't have to be afraid of waiting because we know that God will eventually accomplish everything he has promised to do. The psalmist declares,

Our soul waits for the LORD;
>   he is our help and our shield.
For our heart is glad in him,
>   because we trust in his holy name. (Ps. 33:20–21)

When we trust in the Lord and what he has done for us, "our heart is glad in him." That is our hope—to find our ultimate satisfaction not in pornography (which will never truly satisfy) but in God alone.

WHAT'S DISTINCT FOR A SINGLE WOMAN WHO IS FIGHTING PORNOGRAPHY?

How to Fight against Female Shame

Contrary to some popular beliefs, a woman can be visually stimulated and aroused, and she's capable of developing cravings for pornography. We established this in chapter 6. However, as we also mentioned, the predominate distinguishing factor between men and women who struggle with porn is shame. How do we help a woman when she's overwhelmed with shame?

Help her to break the silence and face her shame. A woman faces a double dose of shame since a porn addiction is perceived as a man's problem. We'll help her to be transparent about her struggles. That's a steep hill to climb, considering how much her shame screams at her to run away. Encourage her to be honest about her shame with God and others in order to drain its poisonous influence on her life. A key to disarming the shame is to tell the stories that "harbor shame" and "attempt to spoil [our] identity as beloved,"[7] diminishing their influence by getting them out in the open.

Biblically equip her. We'll also teach her how to theologically understand and respond to her shame. God's Word has something to say about the shame she feels. Four scriptural categories for viewing shame are the ideas of being (1) exposed or naked (see Gen. 3); (2) dirty and unclean (see Lev. 10:10); (3) rejected and outcast (see John 4); and (4) a failure (see Matt. 26:75). Each category enlightens

140

us to a different aspect of shame. An embarrassed woman's ultimate hope can't be in overcoming her shame on her own but in finding refuge and strength in Christ to face up to her shame.[8]

Encourage her to do whatever is counterintuitive to her shame.[9] If shame makes a woman feel as though she is exposed, dirty, rejected, or a failure, rather than run away, she should run toward the Lord and her church community. If she thinks, "You're worthless," or exercises any other version of self-condemnation, she pushes herself to dwell on who she is in Christ and where she wants to be, not the shame she's stuck in at the moment.

A Sampling of Scenarios

Consider four single women: Charlotte, a single adult with a long-term struggle; Eva, who is hooked on erotica and fantasy; Tieghan, who looks at same-sex pornography; and Martha, who has lived through horrific trauma and is working through her porn addiction.

This not a comprehensive list of potential situations but merely a sampling. The first two situations (long-term porn use; erotica and fantasy) are very common; the third (same-sex porn use) is on the rise; and the last (trauma and porn) is less common than the first three.

An adult with a long-term struggle since her teen years. Charlotte shows up in your office. She's twenty-eight and has wrestled with porn since she was a teen. She's sick of the problem and wants your help.

Neither Charlotte's mom nor her dad discipled her on issues of sexuality. They left her ignorant and unequipped, trying to figure it out on her own. Add to this the assaults of the Evil One. The devil put porn in Charlotte's path at a young age—an advertisement popped up on the screen that required just one click. A friend showed Charlotte pornographic images on her phone. A few girlfriends talked about sexual things, leaving their naive friend to do an online search later at home. In each case, Charlotte never specifically sought out porn; it found her instead.

The combination of parental neglect and unintended encounters with porn led the naive young girl's natural curiosity to be piqued. She wanted to know more. That in itself was not wrong—after all, sexual desire is good. It's something God gave us as a gift within the context of marriage. It was Charlotte's decision to sneak behind her parents' backs and view forbidden things online that was the problem.

What if parents proactively create a safe culture in their homes in which young children automatically come to them to talk about sex, no matter how they first heard or learned about it? How many young people would be spared from the hardship of a porn addiction? We'll think through this more in chapter 10.

As Charlotte viewed images online, the pleasure center in her brain was activated and her body aroused, and her carnal desires kicked in rapidly. The innocence of her initial sexual curiosity moved quickly to the pursuit of more porn. Sin took over as her primary motivator. The desires of the flesh overran her. In a short amount of time, her sin became enslavement.

By the time Charlotte shows up in our office, we've got to treat her porn habit as a deeply ingrained pattern, because she's struggled with porn on and off for fifteen years. To prepare her properly, we've got to help Charlotte to see that over a decade of porn use won't be undone within a week or even months. As depressing as the thought is, she's probably two or more years out from turning her life completely around. We've got to help her to own the long road and then stick beside her.

We help Charlotte to make connections to the pain in her long-term story—her abandonment by her parents to a sexually charged world; the lack of emotional involvement from her father or mother that made her more vulnerable to her addiction. Faithful discipleship guides Charlotte to understand how her escape to pornography involved not only sinful choices but also decisions she made as a sufferer in this world. Like many, she found comfort from troubling circumstances through the escape of pornography.

Charlotte's story—a woman addicted from an early age—will become increasingly common as members of Generation Z and Alpha (who grew up in a world full of technology) become adults. The shame of older generations will be overtaken by the commonality of porn use among women.

A woman addicted to erotica and fantasy. Remember Eva from the start of this chapter? She read erotic literature and fantasized, in her loneliness creating an alternate refuge. She went to church every Sunday, living as a dutiful Christian. But no one knew about the secret pleasures she engaged in.

The addictive quality of erotica and fantasy shouldn't be downplayed. To do so is to tell a struggling believer, "Your problem is not that big a deal." That's unkind and unfair.

Eva's driven by her desire to be desired and by her hunger for male companionship and intimate experiences.[10] From an early age, Eva was wooed by Hollywood love stories and chick flicks that told her that true happiness is found in a man's attention and love. Every playtime, she had Barbie meet Ken and live happily ever after. (Disney never shows what happens later in a marriage, when things get hard!) Now Eva idolizes the experience of being pursued and cherished by a man. If God doesn't provide her with a husband, she doubts God's goodness and love. As Helen Thorne suggests, "We may love God, but we will love the idea of being with a man more."[11]

Eva can work, pay her bills, shop for groceries, and get coffee—all on her own. Though loneliness is painful, she is able to survive without a partner and companion. But it's hard for her to bear up under the possibility of never having sex. Eva yearns for intimacy and pleasure. She longs for the closeness and security that sex brings. If she says, "I'm willing to wait," she can keep fighting. But if she says, "I'm not going to trust God with my sex life," then she's given herself over to the idol of pleasurable experiences.

How do you help to diffuse the power of Eva's fantasy life and assist her in recapturing her heart and mind and bringing them back to Christ? Her inner world needs to be disciplined. She needs self-control, which is a fruit of the Spirit (see Gal. 5:22); the ability to make wise decisions (see Prov. 1:1–7); and greater maturity (see Col. 1:28–29). Self-control is the result of the power of God working supernaturally through the Spirit in Eva's inner being, giving her new strength and the resolve to engage in the battle for her thought life (see Eph. 3:16). Like Charlotte, Eva needs encouragement to persevere in the long process of transformation.

One means that God will use to help Eva is accountability with a fellow believer. Accountability asks a wide range of questions, but especially about Eva's internal world (her thoughts, feelings, and heart issues). Eva needs encouragement and gentle confrontation from a close friend who weekly (and, initially, probably daily) asks questions like the following: How are you calling out to Jesus to help you in these temptations? Did you fantasize again, and, if so, were you aware of God at all before you gave in? What were your triggers? What kept you going this week? What are you longing for in your fantasies? Where are you putting your hope?

To just tell Eva to stop is insufficient. She may need you to comfort her in her heartache and pain before you challenge her with exhortations. Remember, she (like you!) is a sinner *and* a sufferer. She longs for children and a husband; she's lonely on Friday nights when she gets bored and doesn't have a date; she wavers between trusting in the Lord and wallowing in self-pity and self-condemnation. A wise helper asks God to give her discernment for whether she should lean more heavily on the challenge of the gospel or the comfort it provides as she meets with Eva from week to week. To leave these things unaddressed will set her up for failure and discouragement.

A woman addicted to same-sex pornography. Tieghan grew up in a conservative home and developed a strong, romantic same-sex attraction (SSA) at an early age. In her Christian high school, she and another girl developed a friendship that soon became romantic.

To help Tieghan, it's important for us to understand that some girls and women struggle with and disclose SSA prior to any same-sex behavior. This fact informs the role that same-sex pornography plays in their development. It may be a way for Tieghan to confirm, explore, or answer questions related to her same-sex attraction.

Struggling with any type of pornography brings shame. The stigma associated with same-sex pornography is even more significant.

Though there are obvious differences between addictions to opposite-sex and same-sex pornography, the helping principles remain true and useful in both cases.

Help Tieghan to see where same-sex desire comes from (the heart) and to recognize that she can sinfully engage it (succumbing to temptation) or withstand it and run to Christ (growing through trial). This gives her categories to understand herself without either giving in or giving up.

Connecting Tieghan to godly women in her life who can provide a safe and confidential space for her is key. The world tells Tieghan that she *is* what she feels. Good Christian discipleship helps her to rightly locate emotion and feeling within the large context of holiness and obedience. Just because Tieghan feels a certain way does not mean that's who she is.

A woman who experienced trauma and later engages with porn. Martha was abused both sexually and emotionally by her father while she was growing up. As an adult, she gravitated toward porn. Pornography traffics in themes of sadomasochism, humiliation, misuse of power, and women in subservient roles. For many women who have experienced trauma in their past, there is a connection between their trauma and the pornography they watch. The porn industry understands this and "knows that porn users who have endured these traumas will be aroused by the eroticizing of these traumas later in life."[12]

Martha feels guilt, shame, and unworthiness because of her past trauma, and that is what drew her to porn in the first place.[13] She felt dirty and disgusting *before* she watched porn for the first time.

Martha seeks out porn as a way to treat herself the way she feels she deserves to be treated.

Different women react to trauma in different ways. Many people who experience trauma don't struggle with pornography, but acting out sexually is common. Martha watched porn almost as a reenactment or reexperience of her past trauma. Another woman may feel that her virginity or purity was taken away, so it doesn't matter if she sleeps around or watches porn. Yet another woman may use porn as a way to put herself in a sexual situation where she is in control.

Rather than focusing on helping Martha to overcome lust and craving, we pour our energy into making associations between her porn use and her past trauma. As we talk to her in our meetings about her sense of shame and feeling dirty, we help Martha to connect these feelings with specific difficult events or traumas that happened *before* she started viewing pornography. We get her to verbalize and articulate the parts of her narrative that are riddled with shame, but we're careful to do so at a slow pace so we don't trigger reactions from her body.

Then we make connections to what led her to first watch porn. We ask, "When was the first time you felt dirty or unworthy or disgusting? When was the first time you watched porn? What connections do you see?" This often leads to different entry points for talking about the guilt, shame, and identity issues that are concrete problems for Martha. Instead of discussing her life more generally, we look at how her porn habits connect to difficulties and trauma that happened in her past.

Martha needs trauma counseling more than she needs help with her pornography addiction. Her porn use is a symptom of the deeper wounds related to her trauma. As she experiences healing from trauma, it won't be surprising for her porn use to resolve.

A woman may watch violent porn without any memory of trauma in her past. The trauma may not have happened, or it may be buried and hard for her to consciously access. Don't presume one or the other. Your best bet is to get help from an experienced counselor who has worked a lot with women.

PORNOGRAPHY PROBLEMS VERSUS EVERLASTING GLORY

In many congregations, marriage is rightfully held up as a good and godly thing to pursue. Yet singles often are left to feel like second-class citizens in their own churches. The pastor prays for couples who get engaged and married, for couples who get pregnant or give birth to children, for godly fathers and mothers, and for gospel-centered parenting. But he *rarely* (if ever) prays for singles or the good and bad seasons of singleness. Is it any wonder that singles are left to feel secondary?

Though pornography and masturbation struggles are discouraging, they don't have to define a single adult, nor do they have to be a ruling dynamic for the rest of his life. There is hope in the kingdom of God for singles to defeat pornography and masturbation struggles.

The Bible starts with singleness (Adam was all alone before God made Eve), and it ends with singleness (none of us will be married to one another in heaven). When we get to heaven, and there is no sin of pornography anymore, we'll all be single and, collectively, as the body of Christ, we will be married to Jesus, our Groom . . . every one of us. That means marriage is a temporary good, but singleness, without any sin, will go on for all eternity. Glory be to God.

BUILD A RESCUE PLAN

Personal Reflection

Based on this chapter, where do you need to change your approach to helping singles? What things need to change in your one-on-one discipling and your church? Can you teach more about singleness in your church and speak to the feelings and desires that singles wrestle with? Can you begin to incorporate singles more into your family life? Can you ask a few singles in your life about the challenges they face? How can you bring them greater hope in Christ?

Potential Problems

Impatience is a common problem in our culture. How can you help singles to wait well?

Practical Step

On the front end of this chapter, we included a summary of an overall game plan from our companion book, *Rescue Skills*. Pick out the places where you think your discipling is going well and identify a few areas that need to change.

Prayer

Lord, help me to be an encouragement to single adults. Use your Word and conviction from the Spirit to strengthen singles to grow in Christ. Allow me to demonstrate Christ's love and be an encouragement. In Jesus's name, amen.

8

DATING: WHEN A BOYFRIEND OR GIRLFRIEND CONFESSES

Porn is unloving. . . . Don't lower your standards.
—John Piper, *"Is My Boyfriend's Porn a Marriage Deal Breaker?"*

In order to love you, he must fight . . .
and part of that fight will be against himself.
—Russell Moore, *"Should I Marry a Man with*
Pornography Struggles? My Response"

Tears well up in Bella's eyes. "What do I do? Do I break up with Cameron or do we keep going?" Her confusion is plastered all over her face. After six months of dating, Cameron has confessed a pornography addiction, and Bella has walked away from their conversation flustered.

Cameron and Bella met at church. He initiated a coffee date, and they hit it off immediately. They loved to talk, so it was easy for them to spend time together. Cameron was kind, thoughtful, and funny. From the very beginning, Bella could see that he wanted to treat her well.

But she had hints that something was wrong. Cameron was tired some mornings, so she knew he'd been up late. He was often on his phone during downtimes, and it was hard for her to peel it away from him. He showed moments of irritation when she least expected it. When she asked, "Is anything wrong?" he avoided her question, saying he was fine.

149

Bella and Cameron were out for a walk one day when he said, "I've got something I need to tell you." A pit opened at the bottom of her stomach. She knew the time had come: he was about to tell her whatever had been troubling him. Cameron hesitated. With a little gentle coaxing from Bella ("It's okay. Whatever it is, it's okay. I want to hear"), he shared his long and varied history with sexual sin.

Cameron had started watching pornography at age nine when he stumbled onto a porn website. He was immediately hooked. His parents never caught on, and he never told them. He'd had ups and downs. His accountability had waxed and waned, depending on how available his friends were or how busy Cameron was. He'd tried everything he knew to do—installing monitoring software, reading books, memorizing Scripture. It had been a long and exhausting struggle. His eyes barely met Bella's through most of the conversation.

Bella was initially shocked, but she held in her surprise so she wouldn't add to Cameron's shame. She knew guys struggled with porn, but no one had ever prepared her for *this* conversation. Sure, he was irritable on occasion, but who wasn't (especially prior to a gulp of coffee)? In her eyes, the good stuff in their relationship far outweighed the bad. Cameron went to church, read his Bible, and was a Christian. She'd declined invitations from non-Christians and waited for a Christian to pursue her, only to find out that her Christian boyfriend struggled like all the non-Christian guys she knew. What was she supposed to do? Should she stick with him or ditch him? Should she help him, or should she leave that to other people? If he proposed, should she say yes, or should she wait until he got this problem under control? Bella had invested so much in their relationship. She didn't want to give it up.

The impact of porn on dating has its own unique challenges. What do you do if you are Bella—you're not married, yet you're emotionally attached to a porn struggler? Will the problem affect your future marriage, or is the struggle with porn a single person's issue? Unlike a wife with a husband, Bella has no obligation to stick with her boyfriend, so should she get out now? Some of her friends say it's not that big a deal, while others (her pastor, Tom, and her discipler, Betty) insist, "You should break it off until he cleans up his act." What should she do with this mixed advice?

Although there is no one-size-fits-all approach, and every relationship has its own specifics, there are some principles to consider if you find yourself in the same position as Bella or discipling someone like her. She's months into the dating relationship, and he's confessed his struggle with pornography. What should she do?

As we have made clear throughout the book, women struggle with porn also. Later in this chapter, we've included the story of Sharon (a woman who is addicted to porn) and her boyfriend, Ben. We'll start by working through Cameron and Bella's story, and then we'll compare and contrast it with Sharon and Ben's.

SEX, HOLINESS, AND PURITY

A lot of dating advice is rooted in prudence, wisdom, and experience. You are bound to read dating advice that you disagree with or don't think applies to your specific relationship. Nonetheless, as Christians we are held to biblical standards for sex, purity, and holiness, and we need to know what they are.

Sex Is a Positive Good from God

God has designed sex for the context of marriage. It's a gift to a man and woman who have committed themselves to each other in the permanent covenant of marriage. Sex is about more than just procreation and pleasure. Intimacy is a means God uses to foster unity in marriage.[1]

Sexual Immorality Is a Sin against God

Sex outside marriage is wrong because it goes against God's law. It lies about what marriage is; it defames the picture of the gospel—Christ's sacrificial death for his bride.[2] It lies about who God is and about God's good plans for marriage. Sexual immorality is selfish in its nature—more about satisfying our desires than pleasing the Lord. It's also unloving because, separated from marriage, sex exploits and consumes another image bearer.[3]

"Pornography strikes out against the picture of Christ and his church by disrupting the one-flesh union, leaving couples like our prehistoric ancestors, hiding from one another and from God in the darkness of shame." **—Russell Moore**[4]

Porn Use Goes against God and a Future Spouse

Pornography is sexual immorality. It's wrong because it selfishly consumes what is only meant for marriage. Thus, it's adulterous in its nature. It's a violation of God's design for marriage and goes against God's law.[5] It's a sin against a future spouse, and thus it's an offense not only to God but to the person a struggler is dating or may marry in the future.

God Designed Christians to Live in Purity, Love, and Holiness

God asks Christians to love him with every fiber of their being. And the standard the Lord sets out is his holiness—to be like God in all our dealings. No one is perfect, but with Christ's strength and the work of the Holy Spirit, Christians can grow in maturity and live pure lives that are above reproach—in stark contrast to the world's sex-crazed lifestyle. If men and women give themselves over to pornography, they shrink their capacity to see and know God. In that sense, porn addictions ravage their souls.[6]

The Bible sets up our standard for Christian dating relationships. God desires us to live lives of purity and holiness as a witness to the gospel and a testimony to the strength that the Lord provides through Christ.

"Porn is destructive to a man's soul. His capacity to see God, and the purity and the greatness of his glory, is shriveled. It is compromised. The soul tends to shrink to the size and the quality of its pleasures. . . . When a soul shrinks like that, it won't be able to make much of God, won't be able to see God, won't be able to delight in God anywhere near like God should be delighted in, in the glorious pleasures that he offers us in his word and in his world."
—**John Piper**[7]

DON'T DATE WHILE THERE IS A PROBLEM

With that scriptural foundation as our backdrop, you shouldn't be surprised at our advice. We think that men who struggle with pornography should not be dating. We think it is irresponsible for a man who struggles with porn to take responsibility for a girlfriend, and, if they get married, also their children.

Why is this?

First, a life that is overrun by porn is a lie about God and a poor testimony to Christ. Every time a struggler falls into sin, he's saying to his girlfriend, "Christianity doesn't work. Christ is not sufficient." That's no good for either of their souls. For this man, it's poor leadership and a failure to faithfully represent Christ.

Second, if a struggler doesn't have the self-control to resist porn, his carnal desires are ruling his life. Self-control indicates that a man is spiritually mature enough to take responsibility for someone else, such as a girlfriend or wife. Self-control is important not just for porn struggles but for many other areas (for example, financial constraint and emotions such as anger). As one of the fruits of the Spirit (see Gal. 5:23), self-control is a mark of a Christian who is actively and steadily growing in Christ. Someone who does not resist porn is not being led by the Spirit. Rather, he's being led by the desires of his flesh, the temptations of the devil, and the lure of an oversexualized world.

Third, marriage won't solve a porn addiction. Struggles with lust don't magically go away in marriage. Sex in marriage doesn't get a person's lust under control, especially if he's an addict and is ruled by his desires. Some guys quote to us 1 Corinthians 7:9 ("If they cannot exercise self-control, they should marry. For it is better to marry than to burn with passion") and tell us that they're burning with passion and need to have their sexual needs met. The lusts and passions of the heart that go after pornography won't be satisfied with sex in marriage only, especially if the struggler has never done anything to fight the problem. There is a danger that he'll continue to look for outlets, especially in seasons when sex in marriage is not as frequent (such as when his wife is sick or pregnant). That kind of behavior is selfish, and it ignores the fact that the essential rule of Christianity is loving others and putting another's interest *above your own* (see Phil. 2:3–4).

Fundamentally, we don't think the guy who struggles with porn is ready for a dating relationship yet. He needs to wait and focus on getting his porn problem under control *before* he dates. And if he is dating, our strong counsel is for him to break off the relationship until the porn problem is under control.

"Okay," a reader says, "but I just want to date. I'm not looking to get married yet. Should a guy avoid a dating relationship while he's struggling with porn?"

Yes, we think so. We think the point of dating is to find a partner for marriage. So if you are not ready to be married, you are not ready to date.

"Well, then," a reader asks again, "you said men who are struggling with pornography should not be dating. What do you mean by 'struggling'? Does that mean if a guy falls just once he can't date? How many times does he have to fall before it becomes a 'significant' problem?"

When we describe a guy who is struggling, we're thinking of someone who has a *regular* and *consistent current pattern* of struggling with pornography and masturbation. To see if it's a regular and consistent pattern, we've got to know his history over the last six months or year. If someone says, "I'm struggling just once or twice a month, but I've struggled like this every month for the last year," well, that's a pattern. He hasn't kicked the porn habit yet. In contrast, if he has demonstrated a sustained pattern of purity for months (no incidents at all), then we would quickly affirm his plan to pursue dating.

Here's an important caveat: We never answer this question by just measuring a struggler's ability to fight the sin of porn. To decide if he's ready to date, we look at the context of his whole life. If there is any question as to where he is (as there are a thousand specifics to consider in any situation), the couple should seek godly counsel in their decision-making. But if he is living a faithful Christian life—he's in the Word, pursuing relationships, active in church, faithful in his workplace and in his other responsibilities, and overall doing well emotionally and spiritually—then we're certainly ready to affirm him. A vibrant pursuit of Christ, regular accountability, victory against temptation, and a consistent pattern of staying away from porn are a green light.

If, in the context of a thriving Christian walk, a guy has an isolated incident, we're not going to tell him to break off the dating relationship. So long as one fall doesn't turn into a pattern of sin, he's fine to continue to date.

WHAT IF HE'S WILLING TO BREAK IT OFF?

Let's just say that Cameron agrees with us. He's consistently struggling with porn. He wishes someone had given him this advice before he had asked Bella out. Now that he knows the biblical standards, he's willing to break off the relationship and work on his porn addiction. After he's made this decision, what's next for them both?

He needs to make a clean break. He will be tempted to just put the relationship on hold while he works on the issue, but that's not fair to Bella. Neither Cameron nor Bella know how long this is going to take. She may choose to wait and decline other offers from suitors during a breakup, but that's her choice. The godly thing for Cameron to do is to make a total break—to free Bella from any obligation in dating him.

We've too often seen couples say they've broken up, when in fact all they did was dial their relationship down a few notches. In reality, they are still emotionally engaging each other in a way most dating couples do. This is not enough. If Cameron is going to defeat his problem, his primary motivation and focus should be Christ, not his girlfriend. In the recovery phase for an addict, a former girlfriend can be a significant distraction to his growing in Christ and facing his addictive habits. Granted, the possibility that he may one day get back together with Bella is a great motivation, but it's not primary and should never supersede his ultimate motivation—a fervent love for his Savior. It's more than okay that Bella is a part of his motivation so long as she's secondary to Jesus.

She should pray for him. Daily prayer for his soul and his spiritual walk is an indication that she's letting her spiritual priorities take precedent over her relational, emotional, or sexual desires.

She should let the godly men in his life do the bulk of the discipling work. The model set out in Titus 2 is that of older, mature Christian men discipling younger Christian men. That's who should be standing on the front lines with Cameron, fighting daily alongside him. It's unfair and unwise for Bella to be his main accountability. She needs to discipline herself and drift into the background. (Most women read this last sentence and think, "After six months of dating, that's impossible!" With Christ, all things are possible!)

She should educate herself about the nature of this problem. She can read up on it, talk to other women whose boyfriends or husbands have struggled, and let both her reading and conversations inform her prayers. We do have one caveat. If increased exposure to the problem (through reading or conversations) provokes anxiety or even panic, she should get counsel as to how much she ought to educate herself and on what details.

She should keep her eyes on his humility and growth in Christ, not their potential marriage. The ultimate goal of this process is not marriage but growth in Christ. Bella and Cameron may or may not get married. Regardless, Cameron's soul is in a dangerous place if he's addicted to pornography. By the six-month marker of dating, she's already thinking about the possibility of marriage. Stepping back is painful, hard, and even crushing emotionally. Yet her personal desires can't be prioritized over his ultimate goal—growing in humility in Christ. Their ultimate destination is heaven, not the altar. If marriage happens to be added later on, all the better.

WHAT IF THEY GET BACK TOGETHER?

A struggler's goal should be to achieve a sustained and consistent pattern of growth in Christ and purity (for multiple months at least) before he and his girlfriend consider getting back together. They may come back together again when he is experiencing sustained purity and the men in his life say he's ready to take responsibility for a dating relationship again.

She wants to see that he is growing in godliness and experiencing consistent purity for an extended period of time. She needs him to be pursuing Christ, to be in the Word, and to be actively initiating with his accountability partners. He should have a plan for how to fight his sin, and she should ask him what it is and be fully aware of it.[8] He must commit to being honest with her. And they should agree about how and when to talk if he ever falls again. She ought to be an ally with him against his sin.

Nothing short of a vibrant Christian life is acceptable.

"If I wait for this, I'll never get married!" a reader cries. "So many men struggle with porn that what you said is unrealistic."

No, it's not. We've seen dozens of men change and conquer their porn problems. It is possible on this side of glory. What we're holding out to you is God's standard—love, holiness, and purity. And God's standard will set you up for a successful and healthy marriage. Anything short of his standard could mean trouble.

"You should ask your boyfriend or fiancé who is in his life that is helping him with issues of lust and pornography. You should ask him what technology he uses to monitor and block pornography on his phone, computer, and tablet devices. If he does not have a person who is doing this, and if he is not protecting his equipment then you should request that he begin to do it. If you know that your man is taking measures to protect himself against pornography then that should be very affirming for you. You do not have to be his accountability partner or examine his Internet history to be able to trust others who are doing this. A man who refuses to do these things has told you all you need to know about his commitment to purity." **—Heath Lambert**[9]

WHAT IF SHE DECIDES TO BREAK UP?

Let's backtrack to our initial story. Suppose Cameron is not going to break things off. He's not convinced that he needs to do so. He thinks that he and Bella can date while he deals with his porn problem. However, Bella seeks wise counsel from her discipler and pastor and decides that he needs to clean up his act before they continue in their dating relationship. She decides to break it off with him. (We believe this is a smart move on Bella's part and the right thing for her to do.)

Bella should seek godly counsel on how to break things off but in general should

- *Break up in person.* She shouldn't do it via text or email. It shows more respect to Cameron to tell him to his face.
- *Be careful not to further blame or shame him.* It would be far too easy to cast guilt, blame, and truckloads of shame on him for the relationship's end. That does nothing but make him feel like a worm.
- *Focus his and her eyes on Christ.* The reason for the breakup is not just his porn problem (though that is front and center). Ultimately, Bella wants Cameron to have a vibrant love for

Christ. And if she sticks with him, that will only distract him from focusing on his Savior.

After she's had this conversation, she should give Cameron an abundance of space. No phone calls, texting, or emails. She should step back and let him get to work on his problems and his relationship with the Lord.

Breakups are painful, even heart-wrenching. Bella has got to keep her focus on the cross. When God says he works all things for the good of those who love him (see Rom. 8:28), he's including breakups under the category of "all things." Bella must trust that the Lord intends good for her and Cameron, even if it feels deeply painful at the moment.

GETTING INTO THE NUANCES OF DATING A BELIEVER WHO STRUGGLES WITH PORNOGRAPHY

To delve a little deeper into the nuances of what's going on, we offer just a few more questions for a discipler, boyfriend, or girlfriend to consider as they wrestle with whether a relationship should continue or end.

Questions about the Struggler

How bad is the struggler's problem? Is he just coasting, or is he genuinely fighting? We've often found that strugglers have good and bad seasons as they fight their porn problem as singles. Usually they depend on a mixed bag of some accountability, some time in the Word, and some white-knuckling through the problem. Sadly, at the point when a guy wants to date, he's often just coasting and hasn't seriously put up a sustained fight. We've had many guys cry on our couch as they sat next to their girlfriends (or desired girlfriends), recognizing that if they had just taken the problem more seriously at an earlier point, they wouldn't find themselves in this dilemma. Remember, the goal is a regular and consistent pattern of godliness (growth in Christ) and purity (no incidents of pornography) for an extended period of time. If a boyfriend is coasting and not putting up much of a fight, he should make changes *now*, so that his porn struggles don't have to affect a future dating relationship.

Does he live like a Christian? Our expectation is that a Christian should date only a fellow Christian. By *Christian*, we don't mean in name only. A Christian has been regenerated by the Holy Spirit, is committed to the lordship of Christ, and is born again. If we had a movie of his life, we'd be able to tell you if he is legitimately a Christian by the way he lives. His life will evidence the fruit of his commitment to Christ. Is he genuinely repentant? Does his faith motivate his decisions? Does he show humility and godly sorrow over sin? Is he in accountability? Does he seek out mature Christians for counsel? Is he watching good models of faith? Is he committed to a local church? Is he in the Word? Does he love the Word and God's people? If you can answer these questions with a yes, then he's living genuinely as a Christian and is very likely to be born again.

Questions about the Other Party

Does she feel like he lied to her? Does she feel deceived? When a struggler shares about his addiction after some time in a relationship, his girlfriend may feel as though he has been lying to her. What we don't know is what kind of advice he has been getting from other Christians. Maybe someone told him to wait to share until he was pretty far along in dating. We don't think that's a wise idea. To get back to our earlier example, we would have never let Cameron date in the first place. But if he did initiate a dating relationship against our counsel, we'd encourage him to be honest right away. Otherwise, his secret will hurt the relationship, and his girlfriend will feel deceived if he waits for six months before telling her about it. If Bella feels deceived by Cameron, and she feels like he was given bad advice by the discipler, that will make resolving the relationship more complicated and difficult for them both. It will make it harder for her to trust him.

Is she figuring this out on her own or getting godly advice and counsel? It's never wise to make dating decisions on your own. Dating is never meant to take place in isolation but should be done in community. Seek out godly counsel. Bella should talk to mature Christian women who can walk alongside her in a Titus 2 fashion as she sorts through the ups and downs of her relationship with Cameron. Because his porn addiction makes the relationship much more difficult, the godly advice and counsel will be vital for her.

Is she inclined to settle? There are dozens of reasons why a godly woman may settle for a man who is addicted to pornography. For example, her dream of marriage may have such a strong hold on her heart that she can easily override the whispers of her conscience that she shouldn't date or marry a man who is addicted to porn. She may believe that happiness is not just a privilege but a right that she deserves. Or perhaps she's forty-one and has not been asked out by a Christian man in a decade, so she sees this as her last chance to get married. Just because a guy calls himself a Christian, holds down a steady job, and showers regularly doesn't mean you should settle for him. That's too low of a bar. We want to value what God values and trust what his Word tells us is actually best for us. Holiness, purity, true love, and the gospel are at stake—not just a woman's desire to get married. For a woman to date and marry a man who is struggling with pornography is not good for him and not good for her.

Does she have a history with abuse, or did she grow up with bad family dynamics such as a difficult father or a dysfunctional home? A woman who comes from an abusive home or a background with bad family dynamics may emerge with deep insecurities and a poor sense of self. We've counseled women who think things like "I'm trash" or "I don't deserve a decent man." In some cases, the scripts from their upbringings replay in their hearts and minds, affirming their sense of worthlessness. Bella's father physically abused her and called her worthless when she was a teenager and a young woman. Her sense of identity was deformed by her father's abuse. Her mother never defended her but threw in her own degrading comments.

Abuse is wrong. Any kind of degrading behavior toward women—physical, verbal, sexual, emotional—is evil. God hates it, and we condemn any such behavior. The sad reality is that women who grew up in such homes can be tempted to settle for men who are addicted to pornography. They assume they don't deserve better men, so why bother waiting? Every woman is made in the image of God and should not settle for a man who consistently struggles with pornography. She deserves more than to settle for a man who looks at porn. A discipler needs to be sensitive to the issues of abuse, the woman's sense of worthlessness, and her assumptions about what she does or does not deserve in a boyfriend. This complicates the relationship and adds another nuance to your discipling!

Questions about Them

What if the girlfriend says, "My boyfriend still struggles regularly with pornography. I know that Jesus can change him, so why can't I get married to him now?" While it's certainly true that Jesus can change him, no one marries her boyfriend's future self. Rather, she marries the man who shows up at the altar, with all his sins—not the man she hopes he will be *after* he's changed. (To quote Heath Lambert, "I know Jesus can change him! The greater part of wisdom, however, is to wait and allow Jesus to do some of that work *before* you marry. . . . You should only marry a man who is currently winning the battle, and has a track record of change."[10])

How honest has he been about the sin? Was he vague, or did she know the whole story? During dating, when a boyfriend shares with a girlfriend about his struggle with sexual sin, he should be straightforward and brutally honest. He will be tempted to whitewash his sin—to be vague about what is really happening—because he fears her rejection. Powerful desires at war in his heart (pride, arrogance, guilt, shame, fear of man, and so on) can motivate him to hide or be vague. She deserves to know the truth about his personal struggles, whether with pornography or any other sin. We don't think he should share the brutal details of everything he's ever done. Yet he should share the broad strokes in enough detail that she has a clear sense of his sin, and he should answer any questions she may have. If there is any question as to what is enough detail, he should seek out counsel from his pastor or a godly and wise older man or woman in his local congregation.

Aside from his porn problem, what else should a girlfriend know? The boyfriend should share his plan to fight his sin, and, if he doesn't, she should ask about it. She wants to know he's pursuing accountability and has employed a variety of means to fight pornography. If he has not, his lack of commitment to purity tells her all she needs to know. She should break up with him.

Should a boyfriend share about his past struggles with pornography while he is dating? Yes. We think the boyfriend should share about his struggles in the past. His girlfriend deserves to know who she's marrying. Too many women marry a man only to find out that he was vague or hid parts of his past or current sins.

WHAT IF THE GIRLFRIEND IS THE ONE WHO STRUGGLES?

For most of this chapter, we've presented the boyfriend as the struggler in a dating relationship. What if it's the other way around? Sharon has struggled with pornography over the long term. Ben asks her out, and their relationship goes really well. How is their situation similar to or different from Cameron and Bella's?

Similarities

Much of what we outlined for Cameron applies to Sharon as well, because they're both believers who struggle with pornography.

If Sharon is stuck in a regular and consistent pattern of watching pornography, she should not date until she's dealt with her porn addiction. The same standard we apply to addicted men we apply to addicted women. Why? First, Sharon is a poor testimony to Ben regarding the power of Christ. Every time she gives in to porn, she essentially says to him, "The gospel doesn't work." Second, her fleshly desires and shame have too much of a grip on her life. They characterize her more than repentance. Third, she's not shown the spiritual maturity of self-control yet, which is not just important for porn struggles but many other areas (for example, emotions, such as anger; financial restraint; and so on).

It's better for her to break off the relationship and focus on fighting this sin and growing in Christ. Ben, her boyfriend, can be a significant distraction. Her primary motivation needs to be Christ, not Ben. It's okay for him to be a part of her motivation but that must be secondary to Christ.

If they do break up, they need to make a clean break. They can't be emotionally engaging one another while broken up. Ben steps away and entrusts the older women in the church to disciple Sharon through her struggles. Since he has no obligation to wait on Sharon, Ben's free to date others if he so chooses. If he waits for her, that's on him, not her. Her focus is on Christ, not Ben.

If Sharon consistently struggles with porn in the dating relationship, and she won't break it off, then Ben should have the guts to end the relationship for her sake. He can't assume that she'll change in marriage just because they'll be able to be intimate.

Sharon needs to be studying the Word on her own, pursuing life-giving accountability, fellowshipping regularly with other believers, attending church and sitting under preaching every Sunday, and finding ways to serve others to take the focus off herself. If she genuinely loves Christ, these things will be an overflow of her abiding in Christ (see John 15:4–7).

Differences

What about the differences? There is a danger that we can unwittingly treat Sharon like an addicted man, and, if we do, we undermine the God-given differences. Consider two aspects of this.

First, although women, like men, struggle with carnal desires for pleasure, women have a much greater struggle with shame. As we mentioned in chapter 6, women often experience at least double the amount of shame as men because porn problems are seen as a man's issue. Sharon thinks there is something "weird" or "wrong" with her.

Fighting shame becomes a necessary part of Sharon's battle against porn, and we employ with Sharon the same strategies we described in chapter 7 on page 140.[11] (An important caveat: given generational differences, Gen Z and Alpha probably have a less remarkable difference in shame because porn has been normalized among women their age.)

Second, Sharon may not have the same motivations as Cameron when it comes to viewing porn or masturbating. Sharon views porn because she desires to be desired. For years, she's lived with a deep insecurity over whether a man would ever want to be with her. Even on the days when Sharon doesn't struggle with porn, she's tempted to masturbate because it provides temporary relief from the pain and discomfort of her menstrual cycle. This is very different from Cameron.

Our desire is to help Sharon to see and know Christ and to love him more than anyone or anything else in her life. Through the power of the cross, she can experience change such that porn no longer needs to rule her life.

Because porn addictions are so common among men, it's possible that the boyfriend and girlfriend *both* struggle with pornography. If that's the case, then (1) that's even more reason for them to break it off and each work to address their addictions with the help of their own counselors and disciplers, and (2) there is a danger that they would make each other their main accountability partners if they date, which is a bad idea. In our experience, porn strugglers can be soft on other porn strugglers rather than demonstrate the kind of loving edginess that's needed to push someone to face his or her sin and grow in faith.

HONORING CHRIST

If you are a discipler, your goal is to challenge the couple you are discipling not to settle but to trust the Lord and strive for holiness.

Faith in Christ holds on to God's promises and relishes the hope of the gospel. Lest we forget in the midst of dating, this is the gospel: Christ took on the form of a servant, became a man, was obedient unto death, and rose from the grave three days later, having conquered death on our behalf. God has highly exalted him and given him the name that is above every name. Every knee shall bow and every tongue confess that Jesus is Lord, to the glory of God the Father (see Phil. 2:1–11).

Is the couple you're helping bowing down and submitting their dating relationship to the lordship of Christ? It's far too easy to reduce dating to a horizontal dynamic—the boyfriend and girlfriend who are working out their problems. However, much more is at stake here. The devil would like nothing better than for couples to settle—for the boyfriend or girlfriend to choose the struggler who cannot resist the call of pornography. That way, the couple gives up their pursuit of holiness and purity and God's glory and instead settles for their dreams of happiness and a future together.

If a boyfriend struggles with porn, it is for his good and God's glory for a girlfriend to say no to him and instead point him in the direction of the cross of Christ. She believes in the power of God to overcome sexual sin, and he should too.

The same holds true if the girlfriend is addicted to porn. What matters most is for her to honor Christ with her life. Jesus can change her. Her boyfriend needs to break off the relationship and entrust her to God. The Lord has better plans than either of them could ever anticipate.

BUILD A RESCUE PLAN

Personal Reflection

Are you willing to gently exhort a couple to break up if either party has a consistent and regular pattern of struggling with pornography? If not, why not?

Potential Problems

It is far too easy for a couple to downplay the problem of pornography and press forward with their relationship. That's especially true if both parties have significantly invested in dating and are emotionally attached to each other.

Practical Step

If a boyfriend or girlfriend is struggling with pornography and refuses to break off the relationship, take him or her through the Scriptures listed in the notes of the section "Sex, Holiness, and Purity." Don't argue with them. Pray and see if God's Word can bring conviction through the Spirit.

Prayer

Lord, help me to see clearly and to know your goodness. Aid me in my conversations with couples who struggle with pornography, guilt, and shame. Use me to point to the gospel and the hope they can have in Christ. In Jesus's name, amen!

9

MARRIAGE: ONE SPOUSE MESSES UP AND THE OTHER FEELS BETRAYED

It's never too late to change direction if you know
or suspect that porn is disrupting your marriage.
—*R. Nicholas Black,* What's Wrong with a
Little Porn When You're Married?

Do not lose confidence in God. . . . He's in the
business of taking the broken pieces of husbands' and
wives' hearts and making something beautiful.
—*Vicki Tiede,* Your Husband Is Addicted to Porn

Wyatt cradles his head in his hands and lets out a muffled scream. Why? Why does he keep turning to pornography? He knows he shouldn't, but ever since he first started to look at porn around age ten, he hasn't been able to kick the habit.

Wyatt begins an internal conversation with himself that has become all too familiar.

"This is it. This is the last time. I can't keep doing this. It's not fair to Lisa."

"I should tell her . . . no, wait, if I tell her, it will crush her. Our marriage isn't bad, but something like this definitely won't help."

"I should get help. Why didn't I call my accountability partner? I'm such a failure. I'm probably not even a Christian."

"Okay. I can do this. I'm gonna put Covenant Eyes on my phone and get this under control. That was the last time!"

One week later, Wyatt slips downstairs after Lisa has fallen asleep and heads to the living room. In a matter of minutes, the glow of his phone illuminates his face as the rest of the room remains shrouded in darkness. With the familiarity of an addict, Wyatt scrolls through image after image, video after video, looking for relief and happiness.

The next day at breakfast, Lisa says that she woke up in the middle of the night and noticed he was gone. "What were you doing? I didn't know where you were."

Wyatt mumbles an excuse about not being able to sleep, but he cannot make eye contact.

Lisa isn't gullible. She knows what has happened, and she gets agitated. "Are you serious? I can't believe it. You were looking at porn, weren't you?"

Wyatt nods sheepishly. "Here we go again," he thinks to himself. "What's wrong with me? Why do I keep hurting her like this?"

Wyatt's sexual sin has ruined his marriage. His foolishness hurts his wife, and it degrades their overall marital trust. It inhibits Wyatt from fulfilling his God-given roles as a husband and father.

As hopeless as Wyatt's situation seems to him, the gospel can change him and breathe life back into his marriage. Our goal for this chapter is to trace out how to come alongside troubled marriages and how to provide a compelling vision for sexual integrity. How do you break through platitudes and clichés and chart a path forward? As a discipler, how do you rescue Wyatt and Lisa's marriage? What does it take to redeem their plight and give them hope?

As we have made clear throughout the book, women struggle with porn also. Later in this chapter, we've included the story of Rosa (a wife who is addicted to porn) and her husband Justin. We'll start by working through Wyatt and Lisa's story, and then we'll compare and contrast it with Rosa and Justin's.

THE DESTRUCTIVE MARRIAGE CYCLE

A destructive cycle develops in a marriage because of a husband's porn habits.

1. A husband looks at porn.
2. At some point, he either is caught or initiates a confession to his wife.
3. The wife is understandably hurt by his actions. Every time the husband views porn hereafter, it degrades the trust in their marriage.
4. The wife's hurt leads her to struggle to trust her husband, and it inhibits her desire for intimacy with him. How does she take off her clothes, make herself vulnerable all over again, for a man who has been looking at other women?
5. The husband is ashamed because of his sin, so he's tempted to hide from his wife. He gets discouraged because of the lack of encouragement and intimacy. He also experiences moments of anger and self-righteousness toward her.
6. Rather than accept personal responsibility for his sin, the husband may be tempted to blame others ("It's her fault. If she encouraged me, or if we were intimate more, I would be less tempted") or his circumstances ("It wouldn't be so bad if my work was not so stressful").
7. If the husband gives in to his unbelief and justifies the sin, he looks at pornography all over again and restarts the destructive cycle.

Sex is not just about physical intimacy. Its very foundation is built on security, trust, love, and honesty. Every time a husband looks at porn, he takes a sledgehammer to those foundations. He needs to keep at the forefront of his mind the fact that *his* actions *cause* his wife's hurt and discouragement. Rather than blame her and justify his sin, he needs to own that his sin is destroying their marriage. This whole cycle started because of his sin!

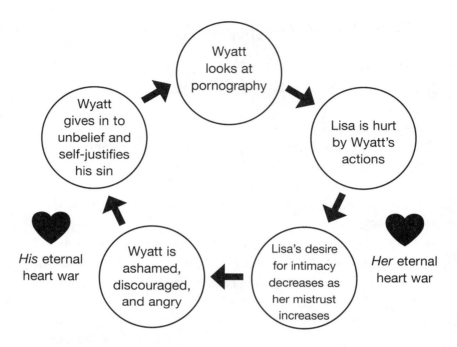

Fig. 9.1. The Destructive Marriage Cycle

Seeing the problem, disciplers think the quick and easy way to deal with it is to get the husband to confess, tell the wife to forgive him, come up with a new plan, and usher the couple out the door. *Don't do that.* Shortcuts won't save the marriage. They will hurt more than help. Any godless solution that rushes to fix the marital problems will be shortsighted, surface-level, and skin-deep. A gospel solution will demand honest work to reveal the husband's heart and encourage him to chase after the Lord. Then (and only then) can he begin to rebuild his marriage.

Let's consider more closely what this looks like.

HELPING A HUSBAND WHO IS HOOKED ON PORNOGRAPHY

There will always be three key players in a troubled marriage: the husband, the wife, and God. We start with the husband's need to reconcile with God.

The Husband Must Reconcile with God over His Sin

The first step for the husband is for him to reconcile with the Lord. His sin is first an offense against God (see Ps. 51:3–4). Pornography, when unaddressed and left to grow like a weed that takes over a garden, can lead him to the pit of hell. A consistent lack of repentance over the long haul is dangerous to a man's soul.[1] So a husband's porn habits and sinful rebellion against God *must* be addressed. The eternal state of his soul hangs in the balance.

> "Her husband [who looks at porn] may claim to be her brother in Christ, but is living in a manner which is inconsistent with true conversion. He is living in a manner which could potentially mean, without a spiritual transformation, he may be separated from God for all eternity. Consistent, persistent, unrepentant sin, shows a heart that has not been washed clean by Jesus' blood." —**Aileen Challies**[2]

Worldly sorrow over his sin causes the struggling husband to wallow in guilt and shame and to quickly fall back into the porn problem (see 2 Cor. 7:9–11).[3] Godly sorrow motivates faith-driven repentance in which he recognizes the foolishness of his ways, turns to God for help, and turns away from his sin. Rather than wallow in his sense of failure, he must trust that the Lord can redeem his marriage. He must not hide behind his shame but must beg for Christ to cover him with a blood-bought righteousness.

The Husband Must Renew His Gospel Affections

The longer the husband's porn addiction has been an issue, the more the husband and wife will both need a long-term perspective. The goal of the Christian is sanctification in Christ and greater maturity. That's a lifetime of work, and he doesn't get to slip in short-term fixes. Porn habits are not broken in a day, but that doesn't excuse the husband's sin. As surprising as it may be, we both know men who struggled extensively with pornography and now, years later, are porn free. Purity is possible in the shadow of the cross of Christ.

So help the husband to start at the foot of the cross, and ditch any quick fixes for his marriage. There is no replacement for a vibrant relationship with Christ. The gospel will disrupt the husband's comfortable, self-serving relationship with pornography and cast his eyes in a new direction—toward loving God and loving others.

All too often, the husband's gospel affections have been long since extinguished under the pressure of a porn addiction, and his carnal desires set the agenda for his life. Hope comes when a fire for Christ is lit in the husband's heart. That's the best long-term plan for him to recover his marriage. He's got to get back into the Word (especially the Gospels) so it can reignite his relationship with Christ. He should not self-righteously think he's better than his wife. Rather, he should follow Christ's example of humiliation and lowliness.

The struggling husband will need to be honest with himself and God about the wretched state of his sex-crazed heart. His carnal desires need to be starved to death and replaced by a greater affection for Christ.[4] We can't reduce his pornography problem simply to a matter of lust. Selfishness, arrogance, anger, shame, and any number of other motivations drive a husband toward porn and away from his wife. There's a wider battle raging in his heart, and the husband must deal earnestly with all the different issues that contribute to his problems.

The Husband Must Relinquish His Excuses and Self-Justification

Viewing pornography is never a justifiable activity. Pornography addiction, at its core, is a worship disorder. The husband sticks his felt need for sex on the throne of his heart and knocks God to the floor. Wyatt bows down to and indulges his sexual desires rather than his need to love the Lord and serve his wife.

Sadly, we run into husbands who wrongly find all kinds of ways to justify their porn habits. For example, Wyatt doesn't feel affirmed by his wife in their marriage. He goes to porn to gain some sense of affirmation and emotional validation, though he doesn't realize this until he starts digging into his heart issues with his discipler, Scott.

Also, as his and Lisa's lives have gotten increasingly busy, their intimacy has slowed down. Wyatt wrongly blames her and says, "She never wants to have sex anymore. What am I supposed to do?"

Unfortunately, Wyatt is not alone in his thinking. Others too are tempted to cast the blame elsewhere: "It's my wife's fault." "It wouldn't be so bad if work wasn't so stressful." "My life is crazy. I deserve a little relief." Some husbands are far too quick to point to 1 Corinthians 7:1–5 but forget Paul's command in 1 Corinthians 13:4–7.

"Now concerning the matters about which you wrote: 'It is good for a man not to have sexual relations with a woman.' But because of the temptation to sexual immorality, each man should have his own wife and each woman her own husband. The husband should give to his wife her conjugal rights, and likewise the wife to her husband. For the wife does not have authority over her own body, but the husband does. Likewise the husband does not have authority over his own body, but the wife does. Do not deprive one another, except perhaps by agreement for a limited time, that you may devote yourselves to prayer; but then come together again, so that Satan may not tempt you because of your lack of self-control." —**1 Cor. 7:1–5**

"Love is patient and kind; love does not envy or boast; it is not arrogant or rude. It does not insist on its own way; it is not irritable or resentful; it does not rejoice at wrongdoing, but rejoices with the truth. Love bears all things, believes all things, hopes all things, endures all things." —**1 Cor. 13:4–7**

One husband said that if his wife didn't fulfill his needs for sex, he was entitled to get it elsewhere because God created his sex drive. What an inverted and distorted way to view sex! God has not designed sex to satisfy a husband's felt needs. (That makes marital sex all about him.) Sex is a kind gift of the Lord to a committed couple, not to the husband alone. Regardless of the reason, the husband should never let his felt need for sex take priority over his wife.

175

No excuse for viewing pornography is legitimate or should ever be justified. Rather than wrongly blame his wife for a lack of encouragement or intimacy in their marriage, a struggling husband needs to own that his porn addiction has ruined his marriage and deeply hurt his wife. His actions are a betrayal of their marital vows and the purity of their marriage bed. He must accept full responsibility for his sin and not pass off the blame. As a discipler, deal up-front with any excuses the husband is making, and clarify responsibility in cases like this—a husband is *never* justified in using pornography, no matter the state of his marriage.

The Husband Must Move toward His Wife

Once a husband has run to God and is leaning on the cross, he can make initial steps in the direction of his wife.

The husband must be honest about his sin. The husband needs to have a conversation with a mature discipler (another husband, a pastor, a counselor, a close friend, a small-group leader) about the level of detail he should share with his wife, but, regardless, she needs to know at least the broad strokes of what's gone wrong.[5] Trust is the foundation of any marriage. Pornography addictions chip away at the marital trust. The husband's goal is to rebuild this broken trust.

The husband is tempted to think, "Ugh, I've got to confess to her *again*?" Yet Scripture demands that the husband be repeatedly honest about his sin (see Luke 17:3–4). If he slips up again, he should tell his wife immediately.[6] Most wives we know would rather their husbands be transparent with them than hide their sin, which is tantamount to lying. Honesty is always the right option (see Prov. 24:26).

The husband must seek, not demand, his wife's forgiveness. Condemnation hovers over his head as long as his wife has not forgiven him, so a husband may be tempted to demand his wife's forgiveness after he confesses. "You need to forgive me." The husband should recognize that *his* sin has ruptured the marital covenant, and thus he must be patient with his wife. More than likely, she's hurt, angry, and confused. A wife's quick declaration of forgiveness could be a work of the Spirit, but it could be that she feels obligated to say she forgives when in her heart she's still angry and confused. Keeping a gospel perspective means recognizing that just as Rome was not built in a day, so also a marriage that has been riddled with porn will take time to rebuild.

"How much and how often you [the husband] should share this struggle depends, in large part, on the health of your marriage. Do you normally share spiritual struggles with each other? Are there other past or current betrayals that will inform your wife's response? As in all communication, the rule of thumb is 'speaking the truth in love' (Ephesians 4:15). Provide truth in a measure and manner that will strengthen the relationship, not damage it." —**Winston Smith**[7]

The husband should show his commitment to the marriage through his actions, not his words. The husband's temptation is to make all kinds of promises: "This will never happen again." "I'll reach out for help today." "I'll never hurt you again." Initially, his words are meaningless in the process of recovering the marriage. The cliché is true: his actions speak louder than his words. For a while, his actions will scream either "I'm committed, patient, and trusting Christ" or "I'm still a selfish jerk."

What kind of actions show that a husband is committed to rebuilding the marriage? He's attentive to his wife's emotional needs; he's servant-hearted and proactive in helping her to tackle life's normal demands (doing chores, cleaning the kitchen, paying bills); he's loving and thoughtful with the children; he executes a plan to fight his pornography addiction without her needing to nag him to do it; and so on.

The husband should reverse any secrecy by adopting wholehearted and complete transparency. Sexual sin cohabitates with hiding, lying, and secrecy. For a while, the husband's whole life needs to be an open book. It's good for his survival, it's best for his fight against the sin that still wants to rule him, and it's a way for him to start earning back trust with his wife. If, at any point, Lisa turns to Wyatt and says, "I'd like to check your phone to see how you are doing," he should gladly and willingly hand it over. The devil whispers in Wyatt's ear, "Protect yourself. Don't let her see your phone." But he has got to override the impulse to hide or protect himself and has to hand his phone over.

The husband must lead in getting help for their marriage. Marriages don't prosper in isolation but in community. A gospel-minded struggler recognizes his daily need for outside help and his inability to rebuild a marriage on his own. The husband and wife should evaluate if he's got decent relationships and discipling, if he needs better accountability, and if he knows how to get everything he can out of the Word. He should turn to godly men in his community for weekly discipling and help. She should do the same—finding mature Christian women who can pour into her. He shows leadership by taking the initiative to find help for himself, by seeking out help for their marriage from a pastor and counselor, and by encouraging his wife to find her own discipling.

The husband must develop and execute a plan of attack—both to fight sin and to grow in faith. He and his wife should scheme about how to cut off access points. They should establish expectations for their marital communication—what to say or do when he struggles or after he falls. They should think together about who should be on his support team and what men (a pastor, a discipler, maybe even a counselor) need to be in his corner.

When he's tempted, ideally the husband can turn to his wife, and they can make a game plan about the best ways for him to cope. He should also talk to the guys on his support team in these moments of temptation! Together, a husband and wife should retool the husband's plan whenever it is not working. Does he understand his heart and the desires that motivate him to pursue porn? Is he broken over his sin? Is he fighting his shame? Does he know how to fight temptation, or is he unsure what to do when it comes knocking at the door? Are his accountability partners following through with what they should do?

The husband eagerly seeks after the Lord, confesses his sin, serves his wife and children, lives in total transparency, and is humble to any counsel and correction. That's his job description in just one sentence.

COMING ALONGSIDE A HURTING WIFE

After Wyatt's confession, Lisa is hurting. This is not a new sin problem. It is chronic. The constricting margins of their growing family, Lisa's homeschooling responsibilities, and her decreasing desire for sex have driven a wedge between her and Wyatt. They are living in the same home, parenting their kids together, and regularly attending church, but, in the busyness of life, they have grown emotionally distant. Catching Wyatt looking at pornography yet again hurts. His betrayal hurts *badly*. "This sucks," Lisa often thinks. "God, why don't you clean up Wyatt? Where are you right now?"

A storm of emotions rages in the heart of the wife of a sexual struggler. Anger, hurt, bitterness, confusion, hopelessness, and helplessness all show up at some point or another. Marriage is supposed to be exclusive, so when a spouse violates the sexual covenant, it hurts down to the very core of the relationship. It cuts deep. Between moments of "I hate you" to "I can't do this anymore," Lisa's heart wanders almost everywhere the thunderclouds lead her. She needs an anchor in the middle of her storm.

As a discipler, you'll come alongside Lisa to sort through this mess. Your first goal is to direct her back to the Lord. Then you'll think with her about how to work through the problems with her husband.

The Wife Must Turn to God and Plead for His Help

In the midst of the storm, there is only one adequate refuge—the Lord. If a wife is angry at God or doubting his mercy, she has got to reconcile with God first before she can look to her marriage. She's got to work on her own heart and her disposition before God, long before the messy work of rebuilding the marriage begins. Her faith in Christ matters. Her faith in Christ is the factor that decides whether she will linger in bitterness or take the initial steps forward. Her hurt, angry, and confused heart is not beyond God's power.

The wife can turn in on herself, or she can beg for Christ's mercies. In the face of another pornography incident, the cross stands a thousand feet in the background, and the wife can barely see it. Her heart and mind are overrun by the folly and damage of her husband's sin. Yet the gospel disrupts and disturbs her hopeless disposition and offers light in her dark moments. A bitter and calloused heart softens under the brightness and glory of Christ. She needs a refuge. Her husband isn't safe, but Christ is always trustworthy. Lisa must turn to God and put her trust in him.

Her prayers may take many forms, but their essential DNA is something like this: "God, this sucks, and I'm hurting. I don't know what to do, so I need your tender mercy right now. Please help me." Again, a gospel mindset directs the wife to look outside herself for help. She turns to the Lord as her refuge: "God is our refuge and strength, a very present help in trouble" (Ps. 46:1). If she laments to the Lord about her plight, she moves her heart beyond the wallowing, bitterness, and self-pity that can be all-consuming.

The Wife Must Turn Back to Her Husband

Once she's worked through things with the Lord and heeded the war in her heart, the wife is in a better position to turn toward her husband. She lets her vertical disposition with the Lord drive the horizontal work.[8] Rebuilding the marriage will be slow but steady work.

The wife should not blame herself for her husband's sin. Her temptation is to think, "If I had only paid more attention to him," or "If I hadn't gained so much weight," or "Maybe there is something wrong with me," or "Maybe he just doesn't desire me anymore." His sin exposes the insecurities of her heart. She must fight against the temptation to personalize his sin. Yes, she has sinned in the marriage, but her husband's pornography habits are not her fault. His selfish choices are *his* sin, not hers.

The wife must not pretend to be his rescuer and attempt to fix his problem. Out of fear that her husband will look at pornography again, the wife may pressure him to find accountability and to put software like Covenant Eyes on his devices. But when she does this, she oversteps her bounds and takes responsibility for his sin. She doesn't leave room for him to take ownership of his sin and repent of it. Rather than do this, the wife's aim should be to support him and show him grace.

The wife should resist the temptation to believe she's all alone.[9] The devil loves to make a wife think, "My husband is the only one who is struggling with this wretched problem." As she looks out on Sunday morning, she sees all the perfect-looking families around her and thinks, "None of them are going through this!" She's wrong. She's not alone. It's a typical tactic of Satan to have God's children think they've got to fight on their own. Help the wife to see through the devil's lies. Ask her to explain to you any lies she's been caught up in. Get her to confess these lies, and challenge her to repent of them. Then help her to soberly and realistically rethink things. (As her pastor, I [Deepak] might say to her, "I meet with the troubled people in our church, and I can assure you that there are plenty of problems around here!")

The wife should share her anger, pain, and hurt with her husband. When they are ready to talk through hard things, he needs to hear how his sin has damaged their marriage and hurt her. It helps him to feel the consequences of his sin and serves as added motivation to fight it.

She should fight the temptation to give herself over to bitterness. Bitterness is like a poison that brings a slow death. It can become a lens through which the wife views everything. She must guard against it by keeping her focus on Christ.[10]

The wife should be careful about asking for all the excruciating details of each incident. The details can roll around in the wife's mind and heart like laundry caught in a constant spin cycle. She may begin to ruminate over the details of his sin far more than she meditates on Christ. That sets her up for trouble.

The wife should be an ally with her husband against his sin, not a cop.[11] The wife's fear (that her husband will look at porn) and insecurity (about the whole situation) make her grasp for control.[12] She's deluded if she thinks that if she knows enough, or checks enough times, or asks enough questions, she can stop her husband from ever stumbling again. She's pretending to be the Holy Spirit, and we know that never ends well. No amount of micromanaging or seizing control will save a marriage. A wife who acts like a mini-god in her own disordered kingdom gives in to fear-driven and controlling behavior. Totalitarians rule by fear and control; wives should never do the same. In all things she is to be Christlike.[13]

"Knowing too much about a husband's battle with sexual lust can create terrific fear and insecurity. This, in turn, can lead to overzealous 'policing' behavior on the part of the offended wife. When that happens, daily interrogations and accusations end up creating more secrecy, shame and marital distress." —**Winston Smith**[14]

A wife should have a righteous anger that's opposed to her husband's sin. Her role is to be an ally with her husband against his sin. She's to be a loving, gracious, supportive wife to her husband. No, we don't encourage her to be his sole accountability. He should have a few mature Christian men who are consistently engaged with his life. They should know the details of his sin (so long as it doesn't cause them to stumble), and she should know the broad strokes of his sin. Yet she should have access to his accountability partners and be able to ask them questions at any point she desires.

The goal of the husband and wife should be to grow their marriage to a place where it is safe and secure and where marital trust and love encourage them to be honest with each other. A healthy marriage is characterized by each spouse's freedom to talk about sin in general (including porn struggles) and eager desire to help the other to fight against sin, selfishness, and the devil's schemes to ruin their marriage. Wyatt and Lisa are not there yet, but that's the destination you can help them to see. They hope that one day their marriage will be a safe place for them to struggle—a place where Wyatt can be honest about his struggles and work alongside his team of supporters to fight back against this sin.[15]

The wife should follow the husband's leadership when he seeks outside help. Seeking outside wisdom and counsel is often life-saving. Solid marital counseling can inject hope where there is hopelessness. Shame may tempt the wife to hide the messy issues in her marriage. However, the marriage is much better served if she is able to open up to a few close and trusted friends about its troubles and her bitter heart. She needs a few godly friends to lean on in the hard times. She should be discerning in whom she picks and speak to those whom her husband also trusts. And she should keep the circle small, being careful to avoid gossip.[16]

If the husband refuses to tell anyone, the wife should go to the pastor, even if her husband protests (see Matt. 18:16–17).[17] Then she should pray that the Lord would convict her husband of his need for help. She must not shame or manipulate him into getting help.

The wife needs to deal honestly with her sin before God and her husband. In the hard conversations about her husband's sin, the wife's own sin emerges. She is tempted to respond to her husband's porn addiction with hatred, bitterness, manipulation, and controlling behavior. Every sin is first an offense against God (see Ps. 51:3–4). She must repent of her sin and reconcile with God.

Early in the process, it is hard for the husband to challenge the wife on her sin because his sin provoked their problems and because their marriage is in a bad place. So, early on, the discipler must be the primary one to draw out the wife and help her to deal with her sin. As the marriage heals and their relationship improves, the husband and wife will recover their ability to talk about her sin in a safe and loving way.

As a follower of Christ, the wife must forgive her porn-addicted husband. Unforgiveness is not an option for a Christian. Even if it is the third time this week he's fallen, she has to forgive him. "But how?" you ask. "Who can repeatedly forgive in light of such foolishness?" Humanly speaking, none of us have the strength in ourselves to continually forgive. Lisa's forgiveness must be rooted in God's forgiveness of her through Christ. Because of the enormity of the debt that God has forgiven Lisa in Christ, she can forgive Wyatt's frequent but smaller relational debts.

Yet we recognize that forgiveness is a process, not just a conscious decision. We think that holy anger against the evils of pornography is justified, especially when the sin explodes like a land mine in the marriage. Shrapnel and debris are everywhere. If the wife is angry and confused, she is better served by taking the time to work through forgiveness so that her proclamation of forgiveness is genuine. We've seen wives rush to forgive their husbands in ways that can be concerning—it's evident that they want to move past the problem as quickly as they can. Maybe the wife is fearful or ashamed. If she doesn't take the time to work through the issues that hinder her forgiveness, they are likely to show up again later in the marriage. I (Deepak) watched a wife rush to forgive her husband. In the weeks afterward, she panicked, cross-examined him, and at times even berated him. She didn't show him a love that keeps no record of wrongs (see 1 Cor. 13:6).

The wife may offer forgiveness, but trust still needs to be rebuilt because of the husband's sin. Let's say the wife has prayed and has taken the time she needs to work through her anger and to extend forgiveness to her husband. She's at a point where she no longer keeps records of his wrongs. And yet that doesn't presume that she's ready to *fully* trust him. We recognize that trust and forgiveness are not the same thing. The husband and wife must do the hard work of rebuilding trust in their relationship. He should be transparent, and she may check his phone for accountability; they should work through hard conversations with love, patience, and grace; he should be proactive in helping around the house and with the children; they should get time together to restart date nights; and so on.

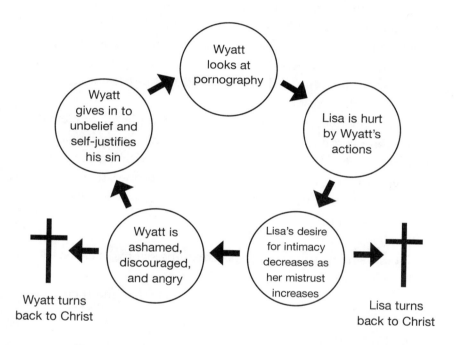

Fig. 9.2. Breaking the Destructive Marriage Cycle

WHAT IF A WIFE SUSPECTS (BUT IS NOT CERTAIN) THAT HER HUSBAND IS USING PORN?

This chapter is based on the premise that the husband has been discovered in his use of pornography or has disclosed it. What if you are helping a wife who wonders if her husband is viewing pornography but doesn't know for sure? Perhaps the wife is struggling to make sense of certain of her husband's behaviors. The behaviors listed below do not necessarily mean her husband *is* viewing pornography, but, when put together, these behaviors *strongly indicate* the use of pornography.

- Does he have a history of pornography use premaritally or at some point in the marriage?
- Does he seem spiritually indifferent to leading in the home?
- Is there an emotional distance and lack of connection between him and her? Does he seem "numb" to her?
- Does he show increased secrecy regarding how he uses his time and financial resources?
- Are there unaccounted expenditures or funds missing from their checking or savings accounts?
- Does she randomly discover that her husband has email accounts, profiles, and apps that she did not know he had?
- Does she log on to various computers or devices and find that their browsing histories have been emptied or erased?
- Does he constantly check his phone? Is he on his phone at odd times during the night or when he's not engaged with the family?
- Does he frequently change passcodes, passwords, and security measures on phones and other devices?
- Does he seem easily irritated or angered by her and their children?
- Does he show increased defensiveness when she asks questions about his purity or if she offers feedback or critique?
- Have there been significant changes in their intimate life as a couple? Either increased or decreased sex drive? Does he push her to do things that she is uncomfortable with?[18]
- Does he suffer from erectile dysfunction during sex?[19]

Go over these questions with the wife. If together you conclude that the husband is likely looking at pornography, one of you should initiate a hard conversation. Be careful not to rush in with settled conclusions, but be thoughtful, gracious, and direct in your inquiry.

"If your partner insists on pushing you further than your comfort level or suddenly has a bunch of new 'ideas' about things to try sexually that are more extreme than usual, you might want to have a talk. On the other end of the scale, if your partner suddenly shows a lack of interest in being intimate or uncharacteristically starts declining you, that can possibly be a sign as well. Also, if your partner has trouble getting aroused when with you, it could be a side effect of his/her porn habit." **—Fight the New Drug**[20]

"It isn't uncommon for porn addicts to experience porn-induced erectile dysfunction. While there are several medical reasons for ED, for the porn addict the problem is not in the organ, but in the brain. They have conditioned their mind to be turned on only by self-sex and porn images. It is common for addicts to blame their partners for their inability to perform." **—Matt Fradd**[21]

WHAT IF THE WIFE IS ADDICTED TO PORNOGRAPHY?

Let's say Rosa is married to Justin, a loving, sacrificial, and godly husband. She struggles with pornography and needs help to fight this problem. How would their situation be similar to and different from Wyatt and Lisa's?

How Is Rosa's Fight Similar to Wyatt's?

Like Wyatt's, Rosa's first priorities are to reconcile with the Lord, to confess her sin, and to seek God's forgiveness and feel assured of his love for her in Christ. If she's acting like Eve—hiding from God, covering herself with fig leaves, and feeling ashamed of herself—then it's time for her to bare her soul to her Maker (see Ps. 51:3–4).

Once she's reconciled with God, Rosa can move toward her spouse. She should be honest about what happened and seek his forgiveness. If Rosa is not sure how much to share with him, she should seek counsel on what's good to say and what's good to leave alone. Her overall goal is to give Justin a clear sense of her struggles and to do whatever she needs to do to eliminate her shame.[22] Justin may be upset initially, or he may run away in confusion or anger. Rosa's got to be patient with him. It may take them several conversations to work through this together.

Not only does Rosa need Justin's help, but she should also go to mature sisters in Christ to be discipled and to a counselor who has experience in working with women who struggle with sexual sin. She and Justin should also seek encouragement from another couple in the church who will walk alongside them and uphold their marriage.

With her support team and her husband, Rosa must develop a plan of attack. She should be thoughtful about avoiding triggers and shutting down dangerous access points. She should be sensitive to her deeper battles—the selfish desires that rage in her heart and the possible coconspirators of lust (shame, self-condemnation, pride, hurt, weariness). She should be in the Word regularly and should sit under the preached Word on Sundays. Her accountability should consist of much more than conversations about lust. She needs help to pursue a rich and robust relationship with the Lord and also with her spouse.

How Is Justin's Fight Similar to Lisa's?

Like Lisa, Justin must turn to the Lord, lamenting to God about his and his wife's difficulties, being transparent about his hurt and confusion. If he's angry at God, he must reconcile with him.

Justin's goal is not to attempt to fix Rosa (as husbands are often prone to do!). Rather, he must show grace to her and support her. His reaction to her struggles can either make them worse (by adding to her self-condemnation and shame) or model for her forgiveness and grace.

Rosa needs to know that Justin is on her side. She needs to know that he's for her and that he'll do whatever she needs to help her to fight her sin. His job description is to be an ally with her against her sin. He can't check out, deny her struggle, or ignore it. He must not leave it all for her supporters to handle. He should be on the front line of her daily battles. His loving and supportive disposition toward Rosa helps her to experience God's grace. He's a key part of her support team.

Justin should fight the temptation to be bitter. When the time is right, he should be honest with Rosa about his hurt and confusion. His goal is not to guilt her but to build honesty into their marriage. Rosa has an opportunity to care for her husband and show him love and grace in return.

Watching porn together as a couple is wrong. Watching an R-rated movie with sex scenes also makes things worse. Any kind of exposure to sexually explicit material is a possible trigger for a sexual struggler and needs to be rejected. Just because a husband and wife do something together doesn't make it acceptable.

How Is Rosa's Fight Different from Wyatt's?

As we learned in chapter 6, women who struggle with porn experience twice as much shame as men. A key part of Rosa's battle plan is for her to fight her shame. Author and former addict Jessica Harris writes, "Shame is in opposition to grace and intimacy. As long as you don't tell your husband, there is a part of you (a very very intimate part of you) that is unknown. There is fear of being found out. There is a feeling of lying, of being untrustworthy. He doesn't know one of your deepest darkest struggles and you're afraid to tell him. Keeping silent might keep the boat from rocking, but it's not going to help if there's a hole in the bottom."[23] Rosa must break the silence and talk about her struggles. She must be honest with God, her support team, and Justin. She should work to biblically understand what her shame is and find refuge in Christ to face up to her shame.[24] And she should take steps to do whatever is counterintuitive to her shame.[25] For example, if she feels the inclination to run away from Justin, she must instead move toward him.

We also learned in chapter 6 that women can have different motivations for pornography and masturbation. Rosa may look at porn because she longs for an emotional connection that seems to be lacking in her relationship with her husband. Or she may masturbate to find some relief from the pain and discomfort of her monthly menstrual cycle.

How Is Justin's Fight Different from Lisa's?

Because porn is common for men, it's likely that Justin either has a past with pornography or currently struggles with it himself. It's also likely that he's helped struggling friends in their fight against porn. If porn is a thing of the past for Justin, we'd hope his experience would lead him to show compassion and empathy for his wife's struggles. He shouldn't rely on Rosa as his sole support and accountability. Although she should be a part of his support team, Justin needs (1) to find strength in the Lord to fight this sin (see Eph. 3:16–17) and (2) to build up a team of men from his church (pastor, counselor, discipler) who can come alongside him.

In confessing his sin, Justin needs to be careful that his struggles don't trigger Rosa's. If they both struggle with porn, their conversations with each other need to be generalized and to show great care for each other. They should be honest with each other, but they need a lot of sensitivity and wisdom to know *how* to have these conversations.

LET THE GOSPEL LEAD THE WAY

Pornography keeps spouses from experiencing thriving lives with Christ. When Jesus is not at the center of a marriage, the marriage inevitably breaks down. A Christian husband cannot serve his own lusts and selfish desires while simultaneously attempting to love his wife. And neither can a struggling Christian wife. She can't satisfy her desires and love her husband. Indulging selfish desires and loving her spouse are mutually exclusive.

Pornography struggles are a serious problem, but they are also a reason for a couple to rebuild their whole marriage from the ground up. Behind every dark sin is an opportunity for the gospel to show that broken marriages can be fully redeemed.

Helpers can offer a gospel-centered roadmap to change by

focusing on the beauty of following Jesus Christ (our true Treasure!); attacking the roots of sexual sin; encouraging honesty and transparency; offering lots of support for the husband and wife; urging the couple to find help from a pastor, a counselor, and friends; refusing to let shame get the final word; and showing an abundance of grace and, if applicable, forgiveness.

Take seriously your role as a caregiver. You are, in the words of the apostle Paul, one who exposes the "unfruitful works of darkness" (Eph. 5:11). Remember that when you expose people to the light of the gospel, you are calling them to the true Light, Jesus Christ!

The apostle Paul reminds us,

> But when anything is exposed by the light, it becomes visible, for anything that becomes visible is light. Therefore it says,
>
> > "Awake, O sleeper,
> >   and arise from the dead,
> > and Christ will shine on you." (Eph. 5:13–14)

BUILD A RESCUE PLAN

Personal Reflection

In order to help a couple to reconcile with the Lord, you yourself must be on good terms with him. How is your relationship with the Lord, and where does it need to change?

Potential Problems

Far too often, couples rush to fix their marital relationship without taking the first vital step—reconciling with the Lord.

Practical Step

Teach a troubled couple the destructive cycle and discuss how the husband and wife ought to *first* reconcile with the Lord. Once they've taken this first step, look through the chapter sections that describe how the husband and wife should move toward each other. How does this troubled couple need to change?

Prayer

Lord, light a fire in the husband and wife for Christ. Reconcile them first to their Savior and then to each other. Don't let the Evil One undermine their marriage. Let the Spirit bring conviction and hope where there is none. In Jesus's name, amen.

10

CHILDREN AND TEENAGERS: WHEN KIDS GET CAUGHT AND PARENTS PANIC

There is no question about whether our children
will see porn. Their exposure to it is inevitable.
—Matt Fradd, The Porn Myth

Wisdom means knowing where those weak points are, recognizing
deception for what it is, and warring against ourselves in order to
maintain fidelity to Christ and to those God has given us.
—Russell Moore, "Should I Marry a Man with
Pornography Struggles? My Response"

Landyn sits at the lunch table while the guys around him laugh and giggle at Miles's latest story. Miles motions for all the boys to huddle together as he finishes with a dirty joke. Landyn joins in their laughter, but he's confused. "What are they laughing about?" he thinks. "What's a blow job?"

That evening, Landyn comes home and takes his laptop upstairs to his room. His mom is shuttling his younger sister to soccer practice, and his dad is out of town for work. Pulling up the Internet browser, Landyn opens a private tab and types *What is a blow job* into the search bar.

Down goes the enter key on his keyboard, and within seconds the search engine pulls up website after website, many with graphic images attached. Landyn's curiosity is aroused, so he finds a link on YouTube and clicks it. Five minutes later, Landyn shuts down his computer, confused but even more curious. He's fighting the urge to open up his laptop again and look around some more when he hears the garage door go up. His mom is back from soccer practice. His investigation will have to wait until later.

Landyn is in third grade.

Your phone rings, and you recognize Mrs. Dunfee's number. You pick it up, ready to talk about the church summer camp program she is organizing, but Mrs. Dunfee launches into conversation before you can say hello.

"Pastor Jonathan, Jim and I need to see you as soon as possible! It's an emergency! Last night as I was plugging Landyn's laptop in to charge, I noticed a browser was still up. I pulled it up to close it out and found a porn website. We've asked Landyn what is going on, but he doesn't want to talk to us about it. We're devastated. We didn't think Landyn was capable of anything like this."

Amelia is at a sleepover with several of her best friends. Karen pulls out her phone and starts looking at pornography. Looking over her shoulder, Amelia thinks, "What's she doing?" Karen notices that she is staring. She holds up her phone, giving Amelia clear view of the images. At first Amelia is embarrassed, but she can't pull herself away. "Is this sex? Is this what everyone makes such a big deal about?" she thinks. Karen notices how much Amelia is fixated on the images. "It's perfectly normal," she says. "Don't tell me you've never seen porn before?"

At home the next day, Amelia gets on her computer to seek out more. She types in *porn*, and what she sees is both enthralling and disgusting to her. She doesn't know what to do with it, but she gets drawn in. Every day over the next few weeks, she seeks out more porn sites. She doesn't want to be caught, so she clears out her web history at least once a week. Her parents never find out.

Amelia is in seventh grade.

At some point, you will encounter situations similar to Landyn's and Amelia's. Conversations about kids and porn can feel overwhelming to both parent and child alike. Navigating a godly path through the mess is crucial. In this chapter, we'll not only equip you for conversations with kids and teens but also offer biblical and practical counsel for parents like the Dunfees. Is there hope for the Landyns and Amelias of this world? What can a parent, youth leader, or discipler do to help them to fight against porn and embrace faith in Christ?

GET OUT AHEAD THROUGH DISCIPLING

We've encountered a ton of parents who are reactive to a problem rather than proactive. The typical parental approach to the topic of sexuality is to avoid the subject as much as possible, drop one big "talk" sometime in their kids' tween years, and then avoid it again for as long as possible.

One problem with this approach is that it's too slow. Parents will be caught off guard if they wait. From an early age, kids encounter sexual content—by stumbling into illicit material online, by participating in sex education at school, through conversing with friends, and by watching suggestive or explicit content in music videos, television, and movies. The world will disciple your kids in the way of sex if and when you don't. Do you want that? We certainly don't for our kids.

What does a proactive approach look like?

"If we want to know what sexual discipleship looks like, we can just take a look at the world. Honestly, they are modeling it masterfully! The world's system has its own great commission. They are doing a fantastic job of converting us into disciples of their worldview and sexual agenda. . . . Our children are barraged by the world's sexual doctrine everywhere they turn."
—**Juli Slattery**[1]

Do Your Research

Who wants to talk to their kids about sex? Awkward, isn't it? You think, "I don't know what to say or how I'm going to answer a lot of their questions." Trust the Lord—he'll help you. Do some reading and talk with parents who've gone down this road before you. (We've listed some good resources at the back of this book.)

God's got a vantage point on sex. He's made it clear in his Word. Dennis and Barbara Rainey offer five foundational biblical principles for parents to use to educate their children or teenagers about sex:

- *God created sex* (Genesis 2:24).
- *Sex is for procreation in marriage* (Genesis 1:28).
- *Sex is for intimacy in marriage* (Genesis 4:1).[2]
- *Sex is for pleasure in marriage* (Proverbs 5:19).
- *Sex outside of marriage is a sin* (1 Corinthians 6:9; Matthew 15:19).[3]

Any one of these texts can lead to a great conversation. Open up your Bible, read these Scriptures together, and start a conversation about what God thinks.

Start from an Early Age

A proactive approach starts from an early age. Sexual discipleship[4] entails teaching a biblical theology of sexuality as early as is developmentally appropriate. Your kids need to know what God thinks before the world gets to them. Disciple them often and early, so that these conversations will be natural and normal by the time they hit the tween years.

Use every opportunity afforded to you in daily life to teach your children the ways of the Lord. Consider Moses's words in Deuteronomy 6:

> Hear, O Israel: The LORD our God, the LORD is one. You shall love the LORD your God with all your heart and with all your soul and with all your might. And these words that I command you today shall be on your heart. You shall *teach* them diligently to your children, and shall *talk* of them when you *sit* in your house, and when you *walk* by the way, and when you *lie* down, and when you *rise*.

You shall bind them as a sign on your hand, and they shall be as frontlets between your eyes. You shall write them on the doorposts of your house and on your gates. (vv. 4–9)

Good parenting thrives in the ordinary, everyday teaching moments of conversation. Scripture emphasizes not only the *content* ("love the LORD your God with all your heart") covered by these conversations but also the *context* ("when you lie down, and when you rise") where these conversations happen.

One family told us that they enter into daily life and conversations with this mentality: "Our role is to prepare them for the day when they are all alone in their college dorm room with the door shut. What are they going to do when no one is around?"

> "In April 2020, the National Center for Missing and Exploited Children received 4.2 million reports of sexual exploitation, online enticement, child sex abuse materials (or 'CSAM'), and unsolicited pornography sent to a child. This represented an increase of 2 million reports from the same month in 2019 and 2 million more than in 2018." —**Daniel Weiss**[5]

Establish That No Topic–Even Sex–Is Off-Limits

Establish in your home that no topic, including sex, is off-limits. It's an awkward topic but a necessary one. Conversations about sexuality are a vital part of discipling your kids—to teach them the ways of the Lord in all things. Have honest conversations with your kids so they don't figure these things out on their own.

One family told us, "From experience we have noticed that sometimes our children feel guilty and don't know how to tell us they are struggling. Simply asking them, point-blank, 'How are you doing with what you are looking at on your phone and computer?' opens up a safe place for them to talk. Even if they don't say anything at that moment, it causes them to think about where they are in regard to purity. And sometimes hours later they will come to us and share their struggle."

Celebrate Biblical Sexuality

Teach your kids about the riches of God's gift of sexuality. Juli Slattery writes, "Biblical sexual discipleship paints a complete picture of sexuality as not simply something to avoid but a great gift to be treasured, celebrated, and reclaimed."[6] Parents should model and uphold a biblical view of sex, not a prudish stereotype in which sex is treated as dirty and disordered.

Be careful not to spend all your time just preaching at your kids about the dangers of sexual immorality. Teach them that sex outside marriage is wrong, but don't stop there. Author and pastor Sam Allberry observes that we can turn God into a cosmic killjoy by implying that he randomly restricts and cuts off ways for humans to be happy. Children grow up thinking that he practices a sort of divine arbitrariness in which he pronounces some things good and some things not good. Allberry writes,

> Every time God gives us a prohibition, he's protecting something good. So we need to teach the positives behind the negatives, and show that God's Word isn't in fact arbitrary but instead points toward what is best and most life-giving for us. Whenever God says *no* to something, he is saying a much bigger *yes* to something else. Unless we thrill people with the biblical vision for marriage and human sexuality—especially how they point beyond themselves to God's love shown to us in Christ—we won't be providing the full spiritual resources needed to fight deep and besetting sinful desires.[7]

We must teach our kids about a holy and sovereign God who loves us through Christ. Sex is a part of God's kindness to us. We shouldn't reduce sexuality to a list of don'ts but instead hold it out as a beautiful part of what God intends for those who love him.

MEASURE YOUR RESPONSE

Let's say you're Mrs. Dunfee, and you've caught Landyn. What do you say or do? When a parent discovers her child or teenager with pornography, her initial reaction is crucial.[8] Tim Challies offers a good word: "I think the default attitude of a parent should not be to really be angry with your kids or really be concerned for your kids. Why don't you see it as an opportunity?"[9]

As you respond to your child's sin, here are some helpful guidelines.

Converse, Don't Lecture

After a child is discovered with porn, the initial conversation between parent and child can be traumatic for both and sets the tone for many conversations to come. Parents need to walk in the Spirit so that their responses are Spirit-filled rather than knee-jerk reactions of disappointment, anger, shame, and frustration. Neither indignation ("I can't believe you did this!") or indifference ("Oh well, it's just part of boys being boys or girls being girls") leads a parent to thoughtful, loving engagement with his child or teen. A timely spoken word can be a joy to the hearer (see Prov. 15:23), and wise words can bring healing (see Prov. 12:18). Don't miss the opportunity to have a gracious, honest conversation with your kids.

Not only should your initial responses be measured, but you should avoid another temptation—to make your conversation a monologue rather than a dialogue. This applies whether you are discipling your kid in general or you have caught your child looking at illicit material. Talk *with* your kids. Don't just lecture them about what's right and wrong. Open up and have a conversation with them.

Be gracious in your attitude and start by asking questions. Don't rush to condemn your child. Use the questions below to prompt you as you think through what to ask or say.

- Did your child or teenager stumble onto the pornography accidentally or search for it purposefully?
- Was your child exposed to the pornography by a friend or a family member?
- Is this your child or teenager's first exposure or one of many?

- Did your child break other rules or guidelines in order to access the pornography?
- Did your child respond with deceitfulness, dishonesty, and lies to cover up the use of pornography?
- What was the nature of the content your child viewed? Soft-core pornography? YouTube nudity? Virtual chatrooms? Webcamming? Sexting?
- Is the use of pornography coupled with masturbation?

In situations in which a child or teen has been exposed to pornography by a family member, especially by a parent or sibling, additional conversations may be required to help the child or teen to process the incident. Being exposed to pornography by a family member introduces additional confusion, pain, and distrust for the child. You can expect questions like "How can my parent be viewing this kind of content?" and "This person is supposed to be protecting me—how can they allow this content in our home?" Parents and youth leaders would do well to be thoughtful, slow, and compassionate as they work through these issues. They should also bear in mind that if a child is shown porn by an adult, this is considered child abuse and is a reportable offense.

Your child or teen is probably experiencing confusion and shame, so she may be reluctant to respond to your questions. Be patient. Your goal is to have a conversation. If you don't get much out of her initially, keep loving on her. Stay engaged in her life. Spend time together. Talk about other things and enjoy sharing life together. Be available for the time when you child is ready to talk with you.

We have learned that combining an activity with this conversation can lessen the awkwardness and potential difficulty. Plan a hike with your daughter and ask some questions. Play a game of driveway basketball with your son and see if he's more willing to open up. Over time, with a lot of patience and love on your part, the details will emerge.

Stay Away from Using Guilt and Shame as Motivators

"I can't believe you would do something like this," Bobby's mom shouts as she grabs his phone from him. "You know how gross this is? What do you think your friends would say if they knew you were doing this kind of thing?"

Bobby looks down, holding back tears as his mom berates him. Her response is understandable. She's shocked at her son's behavior. Yet her reaction is not going to lead Bobby to a place of honesty, vulnerability, and confession. If anything, Bobby will hear and experience this equation:

Porn = Bad response from dad and mom (not pleased)
No porn = Good response from dad and mom (pleased)

Although his external behavior may align with the principles of his parents' desires, behavior that is shaped by a desire to please parents comes at the cost of a more gospel-centered motivation for holiness.

We've heard countless stories of parents who used guilt and shame to motivate their children to stay away from pornography. Instead of cultivating the fruit of holiness, this approach caused many teenagers to sink deeper into secrecy and shame and to hide their pornography usage. Why tell a parent if all it gets you is condemnation and shame? Why be honest if Mom and Dad are angry in response? Guilt and shame keep kids cowering in a dark corner; compassion and grace beckon—even beg—them to step into the light of Christ's sacrifice.

Tim Challies writes, "Our goal is to have the Holy Spirit convict our children of their guilt more than to have Mom and Dad make them feel a deep shame. It is very possible that you are feeling embarrassed or feeling a sense of failure as a parent, and this may lead you to be harsher than you ought to be. Your goal is not to convict your children of their shame before their mom and dad, but to assist the Holy Spirit as he convicts them of their guilt before God."[10] Take a moment and consider for yourself—are you ready to be a loving instrument to help, or are you quick to induce shame? Maybe the

Lord needs to do some work in your heart to prepare you as a parent for these conversations!

Don't Let the Struggler Run Away

Rather than guilting and shaming kids into disowning their porn, parents should invite their children or teenagers to come out of hiding. With gracious dispositions and thoughtful questions, they can lovingly engage them. Get your child or teen to open up and talk about his struggles. Create a safe place. Ask him to be honest. Affirm your love for him. "Talk to me—I want to hear what you're wrestling with." "No matter what you did, you know that we love you." "There is nothing you can do to make us no longer love you." Your invitation and posture communicate grace. "Christ is here, and he will help us."

Help your child or teen to biblically understand his shame. Does he feel exposed (see Gen. 3:8–11)? Dirty and unclean (see Lev. 10:10)? Rejected and an outsider (see John 4)? Maybe even a failure (see Matt. 26:75)? If strugglers can relate to one or more of these categories, it helps them to see that God does understand their shame. But your most important work is to help your child or teenager to see that Christ is a refuge when he feels overwhelmed with shame.

Teach your child to do whatever is counterintuitive to her shame.[11] If shame says, "Don't tell your parents or your youth leader," God says, "Don't hide. Don't run away. Trust me, and be honest." Whatever shame tells her to do, teach her to do the exact opposite. Instill in your child or teen an instinct to run *to* help, not away.

We've spent the last few chapters emphasizing that shame is a more significant factor for women than for men. As we come alongside teenagers in the Gen Z and Alpha generations, we expect a shift. Gen Z and Alpha have grown up with smartphones and the Internet. They don't know an existence without technology. They're also surrounded by an oversexualized culture. They are bombarded daily with sexualized material. And, sadly, many of their parents are loose with their supervision of movies, television, and Internet access. What does this add up to? Pornography and masturbation will be *normalized* among this younger generation. Shame probably won't be more pronounced for girls than for boys because they no longer regard sexual sin as just a man's issue.

Enforce Consequences

When your child is discovered with pornography, not only must hard conversations take place but appropriate consequences be offered. In offering consequences, remember that their ultimate goal is to point your child to Christ. "Throughout Scripture, the goal of discipline is to teach Christlike character, self-discipline, stewardship, self-control, a good work ethic, and service . . . and love for God and man," writes counselor and author Julie Lowe.[12] Matt Fradd adds, "A child who never suffers the consequences of his bad choices will soon learn that he can get away with anything. A child who never learns to respect authority will soon come to believe that all rules and guidelines are nothing but arbitrary standards that can be discarded for any momentary pleasure."[13]

When offering consequences, keep the following in mind:

- A child or teen who intentionally sought out pornography should be treated differently than a child who stumbled upon it. We'd assign consequences to the former, not the latter.
- An older teen who is well-educated about sex and has been given clear expectations by his parents should be treated differently than a young child who is curious and ignorant about issues of sexuality.

When giving consequences, consider that a harsh response discourages open communication. Don't punish a child when he comes and tells you of his struggle. Maintain a safe environment for confession of sin. Be humble and approachable, not harsh and demanding.

Explain the long-term consequences of current actions. Children and teens are shortsighted and prone to live in the moment. They don't consider the long-term. Kids need to see how their current choice to view porn affects their future—it distorts how they view the opposite sex, it fosters unrealistic expectations for a future spouse, and so on.

Lead Your Kids to Live within Boundaries

Recently, I (Jonathan) was asked to dog-sit for one of our pastors while he and his wife were out of town for a wedding. They had obtained a beautiful Bernese mountain dog, Smokey, and built him a new, sturdy pen on their property. The pen had plenty of room for him to run around and be active without running loose and getting lost. Each morning and evening, I would go over with my girls, and we would feed and water him.

On one of our trips over, Smokey raced past the gate of his pen. Over the next hour or so, we tried everything we could think of to coax him back in. I threw snacks into his pen, yelled his name, clapped my hands, attempted a whistle. At one point, I even tried to lift him and put him in the pen while my girls laughed hysterically at the spectacle of their father trying to lift a one-hundred-pound Bernese mountain dog.

Eventually, I did what I should have done all along—I called my wife, Jennifer. She grew up with a lovely golden retriever and was much more skilled with dogs. She drove up, got out of the car, came over to Smokey, bent down and petted him gently, and walked into the pen herself. Smokey got up, tail wagging, and *followed* her in.

What was missing? What had I done wrong? I had mistakenly thought that throwing a bunch of enticing things into Smokey's pen would be enough to lure him back in, but what Smokey really wanted was to follow someone in. He wanted to be led and shepherded. He wanted someone *in* the pen with him.

Being enclosed in a pen is a positive experience for Smokey, not a negative one. It protects him. Outside the pen he has total freedom, but the freedom comes at a cost—he could run away or get lost or, in a worst-case scenario, get killed. Within the pen, he can be cared for by loving owners, while at the same time enjoying freedom within the confines of his area.

Too often, parents believe that restrictions (like limits on screen time, smartphones, and Internet access) will foster outright rebellion. While that certainly happens sometimes, parent and child should not see the restrictions as negative things. They are a loving expression of parents who desire their child's holiness and Christian character development. Julie Lowe summarizes, "[I] can look at boundaries as a hindrance that keeps me from doing what I really want—from being really happy or from _____ (whatever we desire in the moment). However, there is security within boundaries. Boundary lines are meant to be both safe and pleasant. They are the guardrails that keep us safe on the highway."[14]

How do you view boundaries? How do you talk to your kids about them? Because God established boundaries from the very beginning (see Gen. 2:16–17), we want to teach our kids about the necessity of boundaries, as they are an expression of a loving God who protects us. Rather than rejecting the boundaries yourself or letting your kids ditch them, rather than letting them roam free like a dog out of its pen or trying to coax them to stay within the boundaries, can you lovingly lead your children or teens to honor the boundaries that God has established? Maybe you can model for them what it looks like to live within God's boundaries?

What are some examples of boundaries for these kids? They may be limits on anything that might provide sexually explicit content—technology, music, or movies. A parent could restrict the amount of time his child is on a phone or place content blockers on the teenager's computer. The boundaries might be limits on whom a child associates with—like certain friends who are known to be much more free with their use of technology, music, or movies. They may be restrictions on activities that could cause a child to stumble, like going to a PG-13 movie with a group of friends.

Look into Filtering Software and Accountability Measures

Over the past few years, we have noticed a trend toward more and more people treating external accountability measures as unnecessary. The argument goes something like this: "What matters is the heart, and filtering software won't change a heart." While it is true that a filtering software or wireless device (such as Disney's Circle) won't change hearts, it can prevent *access* (one of the four *A*s that lead to acting out). A denial of access can significantly curtail the heart's propensity to give in to viewing pornography. Author Matt Fradd emphasizes, "Some kind of Internet filtering and monitoring is an absolute must. Make this your personal rule: if I am not willing to monitor it, I will not provide it or allow it."[15]

The regular process of monitoring your child's device can be scary and anxiety-inducing. (A parent may fear what his child is doing or fear that his child is doing things behind his back!) These feelings are real and difficult to overcome, but do not let the Enemy use them to keep you from staying faithful in the discipleship of your children. As they should with any fear, parents should humbly give their worry to the Lord because he cares (see 1 Peter 5:7) and because he will meet every one of their needs (see Matt. 6:25–33).

Organizations such as Covenant Eyes have written extensively on these issues and have provided numerous resources to help adults to protect children and teenagers from both deliberately accessing pornography and unintentionally stumbling onto pornography websites.

Don't Bypass the Heart

Although preventing access and setting external boundaries are important, don't bypass the heart of your child or teenager when talking about pornography. Just like an adult's, a child's heart is the wellspring out of which she thinks, moves, and acts. Therefore, we tell our children, "You must 'guard your heart, for everything you do flows from it'" (Prov. 4:23 NIV). While accountability measures are important, we distinguish between what is primary (the heart) and what is secondary (filtering and monitoring). Luke Gilkerson writes, "Technology that merely blocks where your kids go on the Internet (like a filter) can be very helpful, but when we rely merely on blocking mechanisms, we only shape behavior, not the heart."[16]

Too much of parenting amounts to nothing more than managing a kid's sinful behavior. Target the heart. It's the command center for your child's life. Don't just rearrange his circumstances and force his behavior to conform.

One way for a parent to draw out his child's heart is not just to ask about the facts of a situation (which the parent should do!) but to ask heart-oriented questions. Heart questions appeal to a person's deeper motivations and goals. Don't just ask about your child's behavior. Rather, ask him *why* he did what he did or *why* sin appeals to him so much. Then offer to him the riches of a gospel life, in which true freedom is found in Christ. Hold out to your child or teen the beauty of a life that honors Christ and relies on the gospel to motivate and empower.

Remember That Porn Is Not the Child's Identity

When a child or teenager stumbles, don't let the incident take center stage in all the discussions surrounding him. Don't pretend to be a private investigator. Avoid acting like a nervous Nellie. Don't think of viewing pornography as a worse kind of sin than issues such as anger, disobedience, disrespect, jealousy, gossip, selfishness, and so on.

Recently, I (Jonathan) was speaking with a mom whose child had been caught with pornography. In the conversation, she related how disappointed she was and how she couldn't believe her "precious boy" would do something like that. At another point in the conversation, a behavioral issue came up, and she quickly asked, "It's probably happening because he's addicted to porn, right?" While pornography often affects many areas of a struggler's life, it's not the root of his problem, but the overflow of his heart on display.

Questions surrounding your child's salvation come into play here. If your child or teenager has professed faith in Christ, then take the opportunity to hold out the gospel yet again. Help him to rely on Christ, to trust in his promises, to walk in step with the Spirit. But if your child or teenager is not a follower of Christ, then your approach will look different. You can't ask a dead person to walk in holiness and purity! It's impossible apart from the awakening and regenerating work of the Holy Spirit. Does that mean parents lower their standards regarding pornography in the home? Absolutely not! But it does inform their overall parenting trajectory.

If a child is not a believer, continue to hold out the gospel to her with the hope that the Lord will one day save her. Until then, continue to use the same suggestions we've covered in this chapter—giving a measured response rather than succumbing to panic, talking rather than lecturing, being careful not to guilt or shame her, using filtering software and accountability, and investigating her heart motives.

Be careful not to get frustrated when you see a child's lack of conviction of sin or laziness in fighting porn. Parents can't pretend to be the Holy Spirit in their children's lives. When a child falls short (as he will often), parents should not just use software programs, accountability, and investigation of heart motives to help him. Much more significantly, they should pray. A child's stubbornness in sin should incline a parent's heart toward the Lord, who can bring conviction and change where the parent cannot.

PURITY IN CHRIST

What's our hope? That one day, our children will stand alongside us in church, worshipping the Lord, loving Christ more than they love their sin. That's what we want for the Landyns and Amelias of this world. As the parent of a struggling child or teen, you may feel confused and hopeless, but God doesn't. He knows your child, and he's going to carry you through highs and lows, good days and bad, ugly sin and moments of holiness.

It is possible for your child to no longer struggle with pornography and masturbation. Do you trust God more than you trust your own plan for your kid (see Prov. 3:5–6)? Rather than be a cop, hovering over her shoulder, trust Christ. Run to him. Rather than fearing that your son or daughter will stumble again, find refuge in Jesus. Do what's needed to help your child to be responsible, confess sin, and trust the Savior. Under the shadow of the cross, you'll find that God will melt away your fears and your desire for control and show you that he's more than sufficient for these things.

BUILD A RESCUE PLAN

Personal Reflection

If you are a parent of a struggling child or teen, pray through our suggestions in this chapter and think about how you may need to adjust your parenting.

Potential Problems

There are lots of ways that a conversation between a parent and a child or teen can go wrong. A parent may make the conversation a monologue, use guilt and shame as motivators, or offer no consequences or boundaries. Don't let this be you!

Practical Step

Encourage and equip parents. Don't let them be passive or reactive. If you are *pastor*, host a class and Q&A in which you help parents to think about how to get out ahead of this problem and disciple their children. If you are *discipler* or *small-group leader*, talk to parents and challenge them to disciple their children. Encourage them to be proactive in talking to their kids about sex. A lot of parents are squeamish when you bring this up, but don't let the awkwardness of this topic slow you down.

Prayer

Lord, help me to love and equip the parents, children, and teenagers who need your help. Don't let the world get ahead of us. Help us to teach, lead, and instruct our children and prepare them for facing this fallen world. In Jesus's name, amen.

CONCLUSION:
VICTORY, BETTER ENDINGS,
AND A GLORIOUS SAVIOR

At 8:05 p.m., the Rangers responsible for rounding up the American prisoners reported to Captain Robert Prince that they believed the POWs had been cleared out of the prison camp. Prince pulled out his .45 Colt pistol and walked through the American barracks.

"Anybody home? Anyone still here?" He moved from barrack to barrack. Apart from some scattered belongings (stacks of playing cards, a backgammon set, a King James Bible), the barracks were empty.[1]

After a thorough check of the barracks, Prince was satisfied that his Rangers were right. He produced a flare pistol and dropped a cartridge in it. He raised the pistol toward the sky and fired a single shot into the air. Visible for miles in every direction, a flare burst, letting off a red glow and then morphing into smoke.[2] This was the official signal to every Ranger, scout, and guerrilla that the operation was finished.

Mission accomplished. It was time to bring the POWs home.

Do you remember the first conversation you had with a friend who was fighting pornography?

- Oscar was nervous. It was clear he had something to tell you as you met over coffee. After a few minutes of small talk, he commented, "I need to share something with you." And then it all came tumbling out. He'd been battling a porn addiction since he was twelve.

- Lexi met you at church. She'd called the day before to ask to talk to one of the women on the staff. As she opened up to you, she started to cry. She'd been trapped in a spiral of pornography, fantasy, and lust for years, and she didn't know how to break free.
- Nicolas texted you, "Can we talk?" You responded, "Sure. What's up?" You called him a minute later to find out. Turns out his wife had caught him looking at pornography the night before.
- Monica contacted you in a panic. The church's youth leader had called her just twenty minutes ago to let her know that Teresa, her oldest daughter, had been caught looking at pornography on a youth retreat. Filled with anger and confusion, she was at a loss for what to do next.

We could go on. Painful stories of sin and suffering, heartache and confusion. Men and women with no idea how to move forward.

But did you notice? God is on the move. Light is breaking into places filled with darkness. The Lord of the universe steps into lives that are dirty, shameful, and messy and shows that he's not going to let any of his children wander away.

What have we done together? We've covered a basic understanding of sex, addictions, and the four factors that lead a struggler to succumb to temptation. We've thought about the problem of masturbation and how porn affects men and women differently. We've tackled specific seasons of life—childhood and the teenage years, singleness, dating, and marriage. What we've found is that God is in the middle of it all. The Lord Jesus cares. He knows our heartache. He knows the details of each situation. And they matter to him. Every one of them.

The gospel changes the conversations we have and what we do. Jesus is the great Redeemer of our souls. He bears our suffering and grief and the anguish that comes with addictive lifestyles. He takes on the burden of our guilt and shame and the sin that threatens to overrun our hearts. He enters into each situation with grace, comfort, and love, and he changes lives. He transforms hearts. He instills hope. He offers peace.

- After years of hiding, Oscar shared his troubles with his two closest friends—Isaac and Steven—both older and more mature Christians. They came alongside Oscar, praying for and with him, talking with him, reading Scripture with him, and texting him during his battle. It took three years before he experienced significant freedom. There are still hard days for Oscar, but the hard days are fewer and farther between. The gospel grows sweeter to him with each passing season.
- Lexi's bold move to share with you was her attempt to come out of years of darkness. That initial conversation broke the barrier and let Christ step in. It was easier for her to cut out porn from her life than to shut down the extensive fantasy life that dominated her mind. But she did. Years of habit don't change overnight. She faces her fears, daily fights her lust, and trusts Christ more each day. There are ugly days and hard days, but she is headed in the right direction.
- Nicolas came in later that day with his wife, Daphne. The first few conversations were hard as he confessed, and she grew angry. "This feels like betrayal," she said in the first meeting. But Daphne was committed to Nicolas. More importantly, she fought to trust that Christ was sufficient for their worst moments. She wondered, "Can God rescue us? Does he have a plan for our mess?" He did. God had a plan, as he always does. The days that followed started a long journey that has rebuilt their troubled marriage from the ground up.
- Monica moved from feeling confusion as a parent to having frank conversations with her eighth-grade daughter. There was so much pain and shame in Teresa's life, and Monica just never knew. What was initially shocking turned out to be an

opportunity for Christ to shift their relationship in a more honest and gospel-oriented direction. Teresa was hurting and wanted help, and Monica was ready to give it. It took a few years of brutal honesty and side-by-side ministry, but Teresa emerged porn-free and stronger in her faith by the time she left home for college.

The things that took place between the beginning and end of each story differ in many details. Nevertheless, we want to leave you with this—no situation, no matter the details, is hopeless. There is always hope. Because the Holy One and the Beloved Son care, we can step into these messy situations with hope. Jesus is there, so we need not be afraid. We can enter into strugglers' lives with confidence as his ambassadors. God is on the move. The cross casts a shadow on each of these precious people, offering hope to the hopeless. The initial conversations may be fearful, confusing, and directionless. Yet our work, however difficult, is not dependent on how quickly or how slowly it takes a struggler to turn things around.

Don't be scared when messy lives show up at your door. Look beyond those initial conversations to Calvary, and remember that our hope is rooted in the One who can change anything.

ACKNOWLEDGMENTS

FROM DEEPAK

I'm grateful to my family, who patiently waited on me while I churned out this book during the first part of my 2020 summer sabbatical. I'm especially grateful to my dear wife who has read through everything I've ever written. She kindly edited this book, so you (the reader) owe her a thank-you too.

Thanks to Helen Thorne, Ellen Dykas, and Jessica Harris, who all helped with chapter 6. (Ellen was *especially* patient with me as I kept on coming back to her with more chapters and questions—so thank you, Ellen!) It's a much better book because of your feedback and your sacrifice of time to help us.

I'm also grateful to the pastors of Capitol Hill Baptist Church. What a joy it is, brothers, to co-labor with you. I am grateful for the privilege of serving on staff for over a decade.

I'm also grateful to the congregation, who kindly recognize the need for pastors to have a break and get a sabbatical. The church expects me to work hard (and I do!), but they also recognize how often pastors burn out. So they give our staff breaks for the sake of rest and spiritual renewal. I'm confident that I've made it this far because of God's grace primarily, but secondarily because the congregation has afforded me time off. I'm confident this will help me to run the race over the long haul.

What I've also loved is watching our church be so outward-focused—from the numbers in our budget, to less-glamorous overseas service (like childcare trips for missionaries), to hosting pastors all year round. Time and again, I've been astounded at (and instructed by) how our church constantly works for the good of other pastors, churches, and missionaries.

Finally, I'm grateful for Jonathan. Brother, what a joy to see our friendship growing and to have now done two books together. The more I've gotten to know you, the more I've treasured God's work in you and through you. I didn't want this book to be just from my vantage point, so the readers have been much better served by your grace, love, and wisdom.

FROM JONATHAN

Writing acknowledgments to a book is both an impossible task and a task that brings much joy. Impossible because there is no way to acknowledge every person who has contributed to this process, and joyful because to recount individuals' help along the way brings about such pleasant memories and thankfulness.

First, thank you to my wife and family for bearing with me through this process. Many an evening, I would come home talking about this book and the challenges I was experiencing. They remained curious, prayerful, and interested throughout the journey, ever supportive. Jennifer, thank you for always offering whatever was needed to finish the book—whether I was taking time away or coming home late—and for bearing with my weariness at times! I love you all.

Second, thank you to many of you who read various edits and drafts of the chapters as we went along: Marsha Raymond, Joy King, Sue Moroney, Joel Harris, Melissa Affolter. A big thank you to Kolby Thomas, my intern at Parkside Church, who helped me in the home stretch with editing and compiling two of the final chapters.

Third, thank you to my counselees, many of whom read through various drafts and contributed helpful suggestions and even testimonials. This book is for you in so many ways. May God continue to give you the grace to persevere, and may you grow in your love for him each and every day in every way!

Finally, Deepak, a huge debt of gratitude is due you. You kindly brought me along on this project and every step of the way guided our writing. This book would not exist without your aid. You have been a deep encouragement to my soul. At times when I was unsure if we would reach the finish line, you spurred us on . . . refocused our gaze . . . and offered a clear picture of the end goal. You are a treasured friend and colleague.

FROM BOTH OF US

This book and writing was a community project. We drew on the wisdom and experience of a lot of friends, colleagues, and ministry partners. There is a significant list of people who wrote responses to interview questions or read chapters and provided feedback: Kelli Barbic, Charles Hedman, Laura Hudson, Eliza Huie, Jennifer Kintner, Jackie Knapp, Stacy Kramer, Lauren Laster, Philip Leeman, Rosalyn Liu, Hayley Satrom, Elizabeth Selle, Beth Spraul, Esther Smith, Gina Solomon, Kali Thomas, Jaclyn Tubel, and Taylor West.

Thanks to the P&R team for their patience as we wrote this book. It arrived long overdue. But you got two books, when you were only planning for one! Thanks to Dave Almack, Bryce Craig, and the entire staff.

Thank you especially to Amanda Martin and Aaron Gottier. Amanda and Aaron edited *Rescue Plan* and *Rescue Skills*, and through their tireless labors, godly counsel, thoughtful questions, and careful rewording of sentences, they helped us to make them better books. The first draft of these two books went to our endorsers. Because of Amanda and Aaron's work, we think the second draft is even better than what the endorsers read.

Editors are really the unsung heroes of the publishing world, doing Christ-honoring labor behind the scenes. If you ever meet Amanda or Aaron, do thank them. They've probably helped you more than you realize.

APPENDIX:
A GODLY VANTAGE POINT ON SEX

The following principles and observations must undergird your care of believers who are struggling with sexual brokenness and sin.

YOU HAVE TO UNDERSTAND THE PURPOSE OF SEX TO RIGHTLY ENGAGE IN IT

Those who fall prey to sexual temptation often do not have a solid, biblical understanding of sex. Two of God's purposes for our sexuality are straightforward—*pleasure* (we get great satisfaction out of sex because God made it to feel good) and *procreation* (by God's design, babies are the end result of sex). God also uses intimacy to *foster unity* between a man and a woman. God uses sex to create a unique union—physical for sure, but also emotional and spiritual—between a couple. That's a purpose of marriage after all—that the two shall become one.

As our culture tries to disentangle sex from children, whether through outright denial (deliberate childlessness) or murder (abortion), it runs against the very fabric of God's created design.

Sexual immorality distorts these purposes. What God wants no longer matters. What we want, what desires rule us, what idolatry overruns us—all confuse us and make the purpose of our sexuality less clear.

But our bodies and sexuality matter to God. God is most pleased when we seek to use our bodies in a way that honors his design and purposes. As believers, we seek to use our bodies and engage in sex in a way that actively aligns with how God designed and intended them to be used.

Questions to Ask Your Struggling Friend
- Where and when did you first learn about sex?
- How did that impact your view of sex?
- How would you have described God's purposes for sex before you read this section?

SEX CAN BECOME AN IDOL

British satirist and journalist Malcolm Muggeridge wrote, "Sex has become the religion of the most civilised portions of the earth. The orgasm has replaced the Cross as the focus of longing and the image of fulfillment."[1] Many view sex as the zenith of human experiences, the ultimate experience for the human being. Many of Sigmund Freud's theories were based off his belief that we are driven by unconscious sexual desires.

Like many things, sex can get twisted. Good things become bad things when they become ruling things. Satan has not changed up his offense since the garden of Eden—it's still the same old tactic: "I've got something better to offer you than God does!" He takes that lie and recycles and reuses it on us. Time after time, we take the bait and buy into the lie that sex will make us happy, safe, secure, affirmed, and loved.

Questions to Ask Your Struggling Friend
- Where have you seen sex take the place of God in your life?
- Where have good desires (for sex or satisfaction or a spouse) turned into ruling desires?

- What lies does Satan peddle to you in order to get your worship?

SEXUAL TEMPTATION IS POSSIBLE TO RESIST

Jesus modeled for us how to endure temptation, and he gives us the ability to overcome temptation through our delight in him. When we come alongside porn strugglers, we often find almost a *fait accompli* mentality—they've given up. It's as if they've already lost the battle against sexual temptation. But this does not have to be so. Consider Paul's encouragement: "If the Spirit of him who raised Jesus from the dead dwells in you, he who raised Christ Jesus from the dead will also give life to your mortal bodies through his Spirit who dwells in you" (Rom. 8:11). Believing strugglers don't have to give up. The Spirit who raised Christ from the dead dwells in them and "will also give life to [their] mortal bodies." Paul prays and affirms that believers "may know what is the hope to which he has called you . . . what is the immeasurable greatness of his power toward us who believe, according to the working of his great might that he worked in Christ when he raised him from the dead" (Eph. 1:18–20). The power that strengthened Christ to rise and conquer death is the same power that works in the believer. Remarkable, isn't it? God will give the struggler life and power so she can fight temptations and improper sexual desires.

Questions to Ask Your Struggling Friend
- What does the fight against sexual temptation look like for you?
- Have you given up?
- Do you believe that God can strengthen you for the fight?

SEX IS NOT THE SAME THING AS LOVE

We've equated sex with the ultimate expression of love, and in so doing have lost all sense of what either truly means. Our culture sees sex as a mere transaction, and it is normal for people today to view sex on a screen. The message of the Bible offers a resounding critique to such a self-oriented ethic. The essence of love is not sex but self-sacrifice. A Christ-centered sexual ethic offers couples who are covenanted in marriage an opportunity to bear testimony to that mystery. It also offers singles an opportunity to fight for holiness and to focus on others rather than themselves. Rather than pining over everything God is not giving them, they can see God glorified as they live in purity and freedom.

Questions to Ask Your Struggling Friend

- In what ways might you equate sex with love?
- Has pornography distorted your views of what a genuine love is?
- If biblical love is defined by self-sacrifice, how does that impact how you view and engage in (or abstain from) sex?

SEX IS GOOD, BUT IT'S NOT ULTIMATE

For our unmarried and celibate friends, the fact that sex is not ultimate is good news. Our identity as people is not dependent on whether or not we have sex! To be fully human is not to have sex but to fully know and love others like Christ. Counselor and author David Powlison reminds us, "Jesus brings sanity and good sense. He starts by making sex of secondary importance. Sex is a real but secondary good. God neither overvalues nor degrades the good things he has made. By realigning whom you *most* love . . . he makes all secondary loves, including sexuality, flourish in their proper place. That might mean containing sexual expression during a long season, even a lifetime of purposeful celibacy as a single adult. Jesus himself lived this way."[2]

This brings a dignity and normality to singleness and celibacy in a way that our culture can't understand. So it's wrong and guilt-inducing to ask, "Why aren't you married yet?" Much better is the question "What are you considering—godly satisfaction in singleness or marriage?"

In God's kingdom, singleness and marriage are both honored. In fact, even though sex is a privilege of marriage, Scripture unfolds in a pro-single direction![3]

- Singleness in the garden of Eden: nonexistent
- Singleness in the Old Testament: not good and undesirable for a number of reasons
- Singleness in the Gospels: modeled by Jesus, the perfect man
- Singleness in Paul's writing: a gift with positive implications for ministry
- Singleness in the new heavens and new earth: universal

Questions to Ask Your Struggling Friend

- Do you see knowledge of Christ as the fullest expression of your humanity, or have you turned sex into an ultimate thing?
- What would it take for you to make sexuality secondary in your life?
- What would it take for you to move it to the back row of your life (or at least the second row!) rather than the front row?

YOUR IDENTITY IN CHRIST DEFINES YOUR SEXUALITY

Our culture claims that our sexuality is the essence of our identity. Many people say that *sexuality is the core of your being*—so it must be protected with equal rights at all costs. To say otherwise is to invite tremendous pressure from critics of so-called bigotry.

But knowing Christ is our truest and deepest and most fundamental identity. To say otherwise is to confuse and distract from what God intends.

If your life is overrun by sexual immorality, then part of the battle is to reverse this. Addicts' porn struggles can be so protracted and prolonged that sexual sin comes to define them more than Christ. Too often, porn strugglers base their *entire* identity on their immorality. But our Christ-centered identity must define our activity, not the other way around.

Questions to Ask Your Struggling Friend

- Have there been times where you have been tempted to view yourself primarily through the lens of your sexuality?
- If so, how? What is the drawback in centering your identity around your sexuality?

NOTES

Introduction: How to Plan a Successful Rescue Operation

1. For more information, see Andrew Knighton, "The Empire of Japan and the Invasion of the Philippines in WW2," War History Online, November 17, 2017, https://www.warhistoryonline.com/world-war-ii/the-empire-of-japan -the-invasion-of-the-philippines-in-ww2.html.
2. See Hampton Sides, *Ghost Soldiers: The Forgotten Epic Story of World War II's Most Dramatic Mission* (New York: Doubleday, 2001), 85, 88–90, 91, 105.
3. See Sides, 7–12.
4. See Erik Ofgang, "One of the Most Successful P.O.W. Rescues in U.S. History Was Led by a Legendary Connecticut Ranger," *Connecticut Magazine*, October 22, 2018, https://www.connecticutmag.com/history/one-of-the -most-successful-p-o-w-rescues-in-u-s-history-was-led/article_c42d22da-d15a -11e8-b052-eb30c777465b.html.
5. Ofgang.
6. See Sides, *Ghost Soldiers*, 120.
7. Sides, 121.
8. See Edward T. Welch, *Addictions: A Banquet in the Grave* (Phillipsburg, NJ: P&R Publishing, 2001).

Part 1: Know Your Enemy

1. Hampton Sides, *Ghost Soldiers: The Forgotten Epic Story of World War II's Most Dramatic Mission* (New York: Doubleday, 2001), 123–26.

Chapter 1: Sin Destroys Sex

1. Alex Morris, "Tales from the Millennials' Sexual Revolution," *Rolling Stone*, March 31, 2014, https://www.rollingstone.com/interactive/feature-millennial -sexual-revolution-relationships-marriage/.

2. According to recent data collected in a General Social Survey, 20 percent of men and 13 percent of women reported they had sex with someone other than their spouse while married. See Wendy Wang, "Who Cheats More? The Demographics of Infidelity in America," Institute for Family Studies, January 10, 2018, https://ifstudies.org/blog/who-cheats-more-the-demographics-of -cheating-in-america.

3. Nancy R. Pearcey, *Love Thy Body: Answering Hard Questions about Life and Sexuality* (Grand Rapids: Baker Books, 2018), 139.

4. Herman Bavinck, *The Christian Family*, trans. Nelson D. Kloosterman, ed. Stephen J. Grabill (Grand Rapids: Christian's Library Press, 2012), 5.

5. The text doesn't explicitly tell us that they covered their private parts, but we know based on how human beings function now that we naturally cover these areas and feel shame in exposing them. Hence, this is probably part of what's going on in Adam and Eve covering themselves with fig leaves and loincloths.

6. Many have made this point, including Leon Morris: "The Sinless One knows the force of temptation in a way that we who sin do not. We give in before the temptation has fully spent itself; only he who does not yield knows its full force." Leon Morris, *The Expositor's Bible Commentary* (Grand Rapids: Zondervan Publishers, 2005), 46.

7. Todd Wilson, *Mere Sexuality: Rediscovering the Christian Vision of Sexuality* (Grand Rapids: Zondervan, 2017), 48–49.

Chapter 2: The Prison of Addictions

1. Astrid Van Den Broek, "What Don Draper Teaches Us about Happiness," *Chatelaine*, updated June 7, 2012, https://www.chatelaine.com/health/what -don-draper-teaches-us-about-happiness/.

2. Gil Simsic, "Revisiting Addiction Using Depth Psychology: The Myth of Exodus as a Blueprint for Recovery" (master's thesis, Pacifica Graduate Institute, 2012), 12, https://www.academia.edu/4131847/Revisiting_Addiction_Using _Depth_Psychology_The_Myth_of_Exodus_as_a_Blueprint_for_Recovery ?auto=download.

3. See Matt Fradd, *The Porn Myth: Exposing the Reality behind the Fantasy of Pornography* (San Francisco: Ignatius Press, 2017), 122.

4. See Edward T. Welch, "Addictions: New Ways of Seeing, New Ways of Walking Free," *Journal of Biblical Counseling* 19, no. 3 (Spring 2001): 19–30, as well as Edward T. Welch, *Addictions—A Banquet in the Grave* (Philipsburg, NJ: P&R Publishing, 2001), 32–39.

5. See David Dunham, *Addictive Habits: Changing for Good* (Philipsburg, NJ: P&R Publishing, 2018), 19–20.

6. See G. K. Beale, *We Become What We Worship: A Biblical Theology of Idolatry* (Downers Grove, IL: IVP Academic, 2008), 122–23; Welch, *Addictions*, 47–55; Dunham, *Addictive Habits*, 21–22.

7. See Jeremy Pierre and Deepak Reju, *The Pastor and Counseling: The Basics of Shepherding Members in Need* (Wheaton, IL: Crossway, 2015), 74–75.

8. See Dunham, *Addictive Habits*, 27.

9. See Daniel M. Doriani, *James*, Reformed Expository Commentary (Phillipsburg, NJ: P&R Publishing, 2007), 35.

10. Doriani, 35.

11. See Douglas J. Moo, *James*, Tyndale New Testament Commentaries (1985; repr., Downers Grove, IL: IVP, 2009), 76.

12. Moo, 76.

13. John Bunyan, "A Caution to Stir Up to Watch against Sin," in *The Works of John Bunyan*, ed. George Offor (Glasgow, 1855), 2:575.

14. John Freeman, *Hide or Seek: When Men Get Real with God about Sex* (Greensboro, NC: New Growth Press, 2014), 28.

15. Sinclair Ferguson, "Overcoming Sin" (conference talk, Mid-South Men's Rally, Jackson, MS, January 28, 2005), https://www.fpcjackson.org/resource-library/conference-messages/overcoming-sin. See also Deepak Reju and Jonathan Holmes, "Overcoming Temptations," chap. 15 in *Rescue Skills: Essential Skills for Restoring the Sexually Broken* (Phillipsburg, NJ: P&R Publishing, 2021).

16. Adam Alter, *Irresistible: The Rise of Addictive Technology and the Business of Keeping Us Hooked* (New York: Penguin Press, 2017), 264.

17. John Bunyan, *The Pilgrim's Progress* (repr., Peabody, MA: Hendrickson Publishers, 2004), 98.

Chapter 3: An Addict's Four Foes

1. For the first three *A*s (*access*, *anonymity*, and *appetite*), see Heath Lambert, *Finally Free: Fighting for Purity with the Power of Grace* (Grand Rapids: Zondervan, 2013), 62–63.

2. See Daniel M. Doriani, *Matthew*, vol. 1, *Matthew 1–13* (Philipsburg, NJ: P&R Publishing, 2008), 158.

3. These last two paragraphs are a rewrite of a correspondence I (Deepak) had with Philip Leeman on this subject of self-deceit. I have been helped by Philip more than I deserve.

Part 2: Know the Lay of the Land

1. See Hampton Sides, *Ghost Soldiers: The Forgotten Epic Story of World War II's Most Dramatic Mission* (New York: Doubleday, 2001), 168.

2. See Sides, 125.

3. See Sides, 169.

4. See Sides, 170–71.

Chapter 4: Masturbation Is Not What God Wants

1. See "World's Largest Masturbation Survey Uncovers How Traditional Views of Masculinity Prevent Men from Having Fulfilling Sex Lives & Relationships," PR Newswire, Cision, April 30, 2018, https://www.prnewswire.com/news-releases/worlds-largest-masturbation-survey-uncovers-how-traditional-views-of-masculinity-prevent-men-from-having-fulfilling-sex-lives--relationships-300638644.html.

2. One sex therapist, Ian Kerner says, "For the vast majority of men, masturbation is a healthy thing. I'm usually more concerned about a guy who's stopped masturbating—which can be a sign of anxiety or health problems—than a guy who's doing it regularly." Quoted in R. Morgan Griffin, "Male Masturbation: 5 Things You Didn't Know," WebMD, last updated January 28, 2017, https://www.webmd.com/men/guide/male-masturbation-5-things-you-didnt-know.

3. For an explanation of some pro-masturbation views, see Rachel Held Evans, "Christians & Masturbation: Seven Perspectives," *Rachel Held Evans* (blog), June 3, 2013, https://rachelheldevans.com/blog/christians-masturbation.

4. Tim Chester, *Closing the Window: Steps to Living Porn Free* (Downers Grove, IL: IVP, 2010), 91.

5. Quoted in Samuel L. Perry, *Addicted to Lust: Pornography in the Lives of Conservative Protestants* (New York: Oxford University Press, 2019), 44.

6. Quoted in Matt Fradd, *The Porn Myth: Exposing the Reality behind the Fantasy of Pornography* (San Francisco: Ignatius Press, 2017), 101.

7. See James Dobson, *Bringing Up Boys* (Wheaton, IL: Tyndale House, 2001), 78–79. Dobson does list four "harmful consequences" that may concern a parent when their teen is caught in masturbation. The first one is the guilt felt by a young man who cannot quit masturbating. The second consequence is an obsession about masturbation to the point that it consumes the individual. The third consequence is that many times young men are attracted to pornographic materials because of the stimulation it provides. His last concern is that masturbatory habits could later (and most likely) carry over into the

marriage relationship, at which point Dobson views it as unbiblical (see 1 Cor. 7:5).

8. Dobson, 79.

9. See Jonathan Haidt, *The Righteous Mind: Why Good People Are Divided by Politics and Religion* (New York: Vintage, 2013), referenced by Sam Allberry, "Where to Find Hope and Help amid the Sexual Revolution," The Gospel Coalition, November 5, 2018, https://www.thegospelcoalition.org/article/hope -help-sexual-revolution/.

10. See Mark 7:20–23; 1 Cor. 6:9–10; Gal. 5:17, 19–21; Eph. 5:5; Col. 3:5–6.

11. See Fradd, *Porn Myth*, 181–82.

12. Matthew Lee Anderson, "Sex and Sacrifice: On the Structure of Autoeroticism," Mere Orthodoxy, June 25, 2013, https://mereorthodoxy.com/sex-and-sacrifice -on-the-structure-of-autoeroticism/.

13. Stuart Scott, *The Exemplary Husband: A Biblical Perspective*, rev. ed. (Bemidji, MN: Focus Publishing, 2002), 150.

14. See Brad Bigney, "So What about Masturbation?" Biblical Counseling Coalition, May 25, 2011, https://www.biblicalcounselingcoalition.org/2011/05/25 /so-what-about-masturbation/.

15. See Bigney.

16. C. S. Lewis to Keith Masson, June 3, 1956, in *The Collected Letters of C.S. Lewis*, ed. Walter Hooper, vol. 3, Narnia, Cambridge, and Joy: 1950–1963 (San Francisco: HarperSanFrancisco, 2007), 758–59. Emphases original.

17. See Bigney, "So What about Masturbation?" as well as Scott, *Exemplary Husband*, 150.

18. Jason DeRouchie, "If Your Right Hand Causes You to Sin: Ten Biblical Reflections on Masturbation," DesiringGod, December 3, 2016, https://www .desiringgod.org/articles/if-your-right-hand-causes-you-to-sin.

19. See DeRouchie.

Chapter 5: Ten Strategies to Address Masturbation

1. See Jason DeRouchie, "If Your Right Hand Causes You to Sin: Ten Biblical Reflections on Masturbation," DesiringGod, December 3, 2016, https://www .desiringgod.org/articles/if-your-right-hand-causes-you-to-sin.

2. For extended discussions on this topic, see "Targeting the Heart" and "Taking a Wider Gaze at Sin," chap. 2 and chap. 11 in Deepak Reju and Jonathan Holmes, *Rescue Skills: Essential Skills for Restoring the Sexually Broken* (Phillipsburg, NJ: P&R Publishing, 2021).

3. For a helpful supplement to what we are detailing here, we encourage readers to consult "Acknowledging True Beauty," chap. 21 in Reju and Holmes, *Rescue Skills*.

4. Matt Fradd, *The Porn Myth: Exposing the Reality behind the Fantasy of Pornography* (San Francisco: Ignatius Press, 2017), 187.

5. See Fradd, 188–89.

6. See Kevin B. Skinner, *Treating Pornography Addiction: The Essential Tools for Recovery* (Lindon, UT: GrowthClimate Inc., 2017), 48.

7. Winston T. Smith, *The Problem of Masturbation* (Greensboro, NC: New Growth Press, 2009), 12–13.

8. Smith, 16–17.

Chapter 6: The Similarities and Differences between Men and Women

1. Most of this section comes from Helen Thorne in a conversation with the authors on April 28, 2020, and in an email message to the authors on July 18, 2020.

2. See Jing Lejano, "Femme Porn," *Cosmopolitan*, November 30, 2009, https://www.cosmo.ph/lifestyle/femme-porn?ref=site_search, quoted in Matt Fradd, *The Porn Myth: Exposing the Reality behind the Fantasy of Pornography* (San Francisco: Ignatius Press, 2017), 98.

3. See "2019 Year in Review," Pornhub Insights, December 11, 2019, https://www.pornhub.com/insights/2019-year-in-review.

4. See Covenant Eyes' e-book *Porn Stats: 250+ Facts, Quotes, and Statistics about Pornography Use* (2018 Edition) (Owosso, MI: Covenant Eyes, 2020), available to download at https://www.covenanteyes.com/pornstats/.

5. See Jessica Harris, "Christian Women and Pornography: What the Statistics Might Not Tell You," *Beggar's Daughter* (blog), May 12, 2018, https://beggarsdaughter.com/christian-women-and-pornography-what-the-statistics-might-not-tell-you/.

6. Harris.

7. See Megan K. Mass and Shannamar Dewey, "Internet Pornography Use Among Collegiate Women: Gender Attitudes, Body Monitoring, and Sexual Behavior," SAGE, July 2, 2018, https://journals.sagepub.com/doi/full/10.1177/2158244018786640.

8. Quoted in Kayt Sukel, "The Neuroscience of Porn Viewing," *HuffPost*, March 26, 2013, https://www.huffpost.com/entry/the-neuroscience-of-porn-viewing_b_2955650.

9. See Fradd, *Porn Myth*, 96.

10. See Sukel, "The Neuroscience of Porn Viewing."

11. See Fradd, *Porn Myth*, 96.

12. Isak Ladegaard, "Let's Use Porn to Change Sexual Behavior," *Science Norway*, June 30, 2012, https://sciencenorway.no/behaviour-forskningno-norway/lets -use-porn-to-change-sexual-behaviour/1373669. Quoted in Fradd, 95.

13. Ellen Mary Dykas, in an interview with Deepak Reju, April 20, 2020.

14. Jessica Harris, email message to Deepak Reju, April 30, 2020.

15. Helen Thorne, *Purity Is Possible: How to Live Free of the Fantasy Trap* (Epsom, UK: Good Book Company, 2014), 22.

16. Thorne, 23.

17. Ellen Mary Dykas, in an interview with Deepak Reju, May 2020.

18. Jay Stringer, "Silence: The Sound of Female Sexual Shame," Covenant Eyes, October 26, 2017, https://www.covenanteyes.com/2017/10/26/silence-the -sound-of-female-sexual-shame/.

19. See Stringer.

20. I (Deepak) have learned a lot from Jessica Harris both through personal correspondence and her writings. The initial seeds for this idea come from her, through I've developed it in this section.

21. Jennifer Kintner, email message to Deepak Reju and Jonathan Holmes, April 17, 2021.

22. See Fradd, *Porn Myth*, 123.

23. See Paul Bentley, "'Mummy Porn' Fifty Shades of Grey Outstrips Harry Potter to Become Fastest Selling Paperback of All Time," *Daily Mail*, June 17, 2012, https://www.dailymail.co.uk/news/article-2160862/Fifty-Shades -Of-Grey-book-outstrips-Harry-Potter-fastest-selling-paperback-time.html.

24. Alexandra Alter, "The Evolution of E. L. James," *New York Times*, April 12, 2019, https://www.nytimes.com/2019/04/12/books/el-james-the-mister-fifty -shades.html.

25. Helen Thorne, in an interview with Deepak Reju, April 28, 2020.

26. Stephanie Burt, "The Promise and Potential of Fan Fiction," *The New Yorker*, August 23, 2017, https://www.newyorker.com/books/page-turner/the-promise -and-potential-of-fan-fiction.

27. See Morgan Leigh Davies, "A Brief History of Slash," *The Toast*, September 19, 2013, https://the-toast.net/2013/09/19/brief-history-slash/. Quoted in Fradd, *Porn Myth*, 126–27.

28. Philip Leeman, email message to Deepak Reju, May 4, 2021.

29. Gina Solomon used her counseling experience and wisdom to help me (Deepak) come up with these reasons.
30. Philip Leeman, email message to Deepak Reju, May 4, 2021.
31. Jessica Harris, "Women and Pornography: Three Ways You're Probably Not Helping," *Beggar's Daughter* (blog), December 7, 2018, https://beggarsdaughter.com/women-pornography-not-helping/.
32. Jessica Harris, "Can Resources for Men Help Women Recover?" *Beggar's Daughter* (blog), October 26, 2019, https://beggarsdaughter.com/resources-men-help-women-recover/.
33. Harris.
34. Jessica Harris, "The Questions We Need to Be Asking about Female Porn Addiction," *Beggar's Daughter* (blog), May 25, 2018, https://beggarsdaughter.com/resources-men-help-women-recover/.
35. Jessica Harris, email message to Deepak Reju, August 1, 2020.
36. See Fradd, *Porn Myth*, 126.
37. See Natasha Velez, Gabrielle Fonrouge, and Natalie O'Neil, "'Fifty Shades of Grey' Whips Sex-Toy Sales into a Frenzy," *New York Post*, February 14, 2015, https://nypost.com/2015/02/14/fifty-shades-of-grey-whips-sex-toy-sales-into-a-frenzy/. Referenced in Fradd, 127.
38. See William P. Smith, *Parenting with Words of Grace: Building Relationships with Your Children One Conversation at a Time* (Wheaton, IL: Crossway, 2019), 17–18.

Part 3: Rescue the Prisoner

1. See Gordon L. Rottman, *The Cabanatuan Prison Raid: The Philippines 1945* (Oxford, UK: Osprey Publishing, 2009), 48, as well as Hampton Sides, *Ghost Soldiers: The Forgotten Epic Story of World War II's Most Dramatic Mission* (New York: Doubleday, 2001), 256.
2. See Sides, *Ghost Soldiers*, 271, and Rottman, *Cabanatuan Prison Raid*, 49.
3. See Sides, 272–73.
4. Sides, 274.

Chapter 7: Singleness: The Plight and Possibilities for Singles

1. This idea of theaters and sexual sin comes from David Powlison, *Making All Things New: Restoring Joy to the Sexually Broken* (Wheaton, IL: Crossway, 2017), 69–70. The chapter containing those pages—chapter 6, "Renewal Is a Wider Battle"—is one of my (Deepak's) all-time favorite chapters

that David has written. It's well worth your time if you do any pastoral counseling.

2. David Dunham, "Pornography and Sanctification," *Pastor Dave Online* (blog), March 25, 2015, https://pastordaveonline.org/2015/03/25/pornography-and -sanctification/.

3. Hayley Satrom, email message to Deepak Reju, May 4, 2021.

4. Gina Solomon, email message to Deepak Reju, May 4, 2021.

5. Charles Hedman, email message to Deepak Reju, May 4, 2021.

6. For more on this topic, see Ellen Dykas, *Your Dating Relationship and Your Sexual Past: How Much to Share* (Greensboro, NC: New Growth Press, 2019).

7. Jay Stringer, *Unwanted: How Sexual Brokenness Reveals Our Way to Healing* (Colorado Springs: NavPress, 2018), 147. See also pages 145–46 for the idea of facing shame in general.

8. To learn more about a biblical approach to shame, see Edward T. Welch, *Shame Interrupted: How God Lifts the Pain of Worthlessness and Rejection* (Greensboro, NC: New Growth Press, 2012). We cover the biblical categories of shame in Reju and Holmes, "Understanding Guilt and Shame," chapter 18 in Deepak Reju and Jonathan D. Holmes, *Rescue Skills: Essential Skills for Restoring the Sexually Broken* (Phillipsburg, NJ: P&R Publishing, 2021.

9. See Stringer, *Unwanted*, 149.

10. Eva's struggles are merely a small sampling of the reasons why a woman might struggle with erotica or fantasy. For a deeper look at more of the reasons this can happen, see Helen Thorne, *Purity Is Possible: How to Live Free of the Fantasy Trap* (Epsom, UK: Good Book Company, 2014), 35–44.

11. Thorne, 36.

12. Stringer, *Unwanted*, 60.

13. Thank you to Esther Smith for helping us with this scenario. Much of this subsection comes from an email message from Esther to both authors on April 12, 2021, as well as a later conversation.

Chapter 8: Dating: When a Boyfriend or Girlfriend Confesses

1. See Genesis 1:26–28; 2:23–24; Mark 10:6–9.

2. See Russell Moore, "Should I Marry a Man with Pornography Struggles? My Response," *Russell Moore* (blog), January 23, 2012. https://www.russellmoore .com/2012/01/23/should-i-marry-a-man-with-pornography-struggles-my -response/ Accessed July 3, 2020.

3. See Prov. 6:20–7:27; 1 Cor. 6:9–20; 1 Thess. 4:3–7.

4. Moore, "Should I Marry a Man with Pornography Struggles?"

5. See Prov. 5:15–23; Matt. 5:27–30; Rom. 13:13–14; Gal. 5:16–19.

6. See Prov. 6:32–33; Matt. 5:8; Mark 12:28–30; Rom. 13:14; 2 Tim. 2:21; 1 Peter 1:15–16.

7. John Piper, "Is My Boyfriend's Porn a Marriage Deal Breaker?" DesiringGod, June 28, 2013, https://www.desiringgod.org/interviews/is-my-boyfriends-porn-a-marriage-deal-breaker.

8. See Heath Lambert, "Should a Woman Marry a Man Who Has a Problem with Pornography?" *Journal of Biblical Manhood and Womanhood* 18, no. 2 (Fall 2013): 16–17, https://cbmw.org/wp-content/uploads/2014/01/06-Lambert-Article.pdf.

9. Lambert, 17.

10. Lambert, 16–17, emphasis added.

11. The reader will also want to look at chapter 18, "Understanding Guilt and Shame," in *Rescue Skills*. We address how to think biblical about shame and how Christ helps us in our shame.

Chapter 9: Marriage: One Spouse Messes Up and the Other Feels Betrayed

1. See Aileen Challies, "When She Says, 'My Husband Has Been Looking at Porn,'" The Gospel Coalition, February 19, 2018, https://ca.thegospelcoalition.org/article/says-husband-looking-porn/.

2. Challies.

3. For more on these dynamics, see "Discerning Fake Repentance" and "Encouraging Genuine Repentance," chap. 9 and chap. 10 in Deepak Reju and Jonathan D. Holmes, *Rescue Skills: Essential Skills for Restoring the Sexually Broken* (Phillipsburg, NJ: P&R Publishing, 2021).

4. For more details, see "Killing or Replacing Bad Desires," chap. 16 in Reju and Holmes, *Rescue Skills*.

5. See Winston Smith, *The Problem with Masturbation* (Greensboro, NC: New Growth Press, 2009), 15.

6. See Vicki Tiede, *Your Husband Is Addicted to Porn* (Greensboro, NC: New Growth Press, 2013), 18.

7. Smith, *Problem with Masturbation*, 15.

8. See Sherry Allchin, "Help! I Just Discovered My Husband Is Looking at Pornography!" Biblical Counseling Coalition, February 18, 2013, https://www.biblicalcounselingcoalition.org/2013/02/18/help-i-just-discovered-my-husband-is-looking-at-pornography/.

9. Stacy Reaoch, "When Your Husband Is Addicted to Porn," The Gospel Coalition, December 28, 2016, https://www.thegospelcoalition.org/article/when-your-husband-is-addicted-to-porn/.
10. See Brian Croft, *Help! He's Struggling with Pornography* (Leominster, UK: Day One Publications, 2010), 52.
11. See Heath Lambert, *Finally Free: Fighting for Purity with the Power of Grace* (Grand Rapids: Zondervan, 2013), 171–73.
12. See Smith, *Problem with Masturbation*, 14–15.
13. See Challies, "When She Says, 'My Husband Has Been Looking at Porn.'"
14. Smith, 14–15.
15. We got the phrase *safe place to struggle* from Jessica Harris's article "Porn and Marriage: Should I Get Married If I'm Addicted to Porn?" *Beggar's Daughter* (blog), February 6, 2021, https://beggarsdaughter.com/get-married-addicted-porn/. Jessica does a great job describing what healthy communication looks like in a marriage characterized by honesty and grace.
16. See Allchin, "Help!"
17. See Reaoch, "When Your Husband Is Addicted to Porn."
18. See "How to Tell If Your Partner Is Struggling with Porn and What to Do If They Are," Fight the New Drug, December 7, 2020, https://fightthenewdrug.org/how-to-tell-if-your-boyfriend-is-watching-porn/.
19. See Matt Fradd, "Does Porn Cause Erectile Disfunction?" Covenant Eyes, February 27, 2015, https://www.covenanteyes.com/2015/02/27/porn-cause-erectile-dysfunction/.
20. "How to Tell If Your Partner Is Struggling with Porn."
21. Matt Fradd, "10 Signs of Porn Addiction: Do These Describe Your Husband?" Covenant Eyes, August 21, 2015, https://www.covenanteyes.com/2015/08/21/10-signs-of-porn-addiction-do-these-describe-your-husband/.
22. See Jessica Harris, "Porn and Marriage: How Do I Tell My Husband I Struggle with Porn?" *Beggar's Daughter* (blog), March 13, 2021, https://beggarsdaughter.com/tell-husband-struggle-porn/.
23. Harris, "How Do I Tell My Husband?"
24. For an extended discussion of how the Bible explains shame, see "Understanding Guilt and Shame," chap. 18 in Reju and Holmes, *Rescue Skills*. An embarrassed woman's ultimate hope can't be in overcoming her shame on her own, but in finding refuge and strength in Christ to face up to her shame.
25. See Jay Stringer, *Unwanted: How Sexual Brokenness Reveals Our Way to Healing* (Colorado Springs: NavPress, 2018), 149.

Chapter 10: Children and Teenagers: When Kids Get Caught and Parents Panic

1. Juli Slattery, "Sexual Discipleship®: What Is It, and Why Is it Important?" Authentic Intimacy, last updated April 28, 2021, https://www.authentic intimacy.com/resources/2641/the-importance-of-sexual-discipleship. See also Juli Slattery, *Rethinking Sexuality: God's Design and Why It Matters* (New York: Multnomah, 2018).

2. See also Song of Solomon 1:2; 4:10–11.

3. Dennis and Barbara Rainey, "How to Teach Your Kids about Sex," *Challies* (blog), May 29, 2017, https://www.challies.com/sponsored/how-to-teach -your-kids-about-sex/. Emphasis in original.

4. This term is from Slattery, "Sexual Discipleship.®"

5. Daniel Weiss, "Your Kids Have Probably Seen Porn, and You Need to Talk to Them about It," *The Federalist*, June 14, 2021, https://thefederalist .com/2021/06/14/your-kids-have-probably-seen-porn-and-you-need-to-talk -to-them-about-it/.

6. Slattery, "Importance of Sexual Discipleship." See also Slattery, *Rethinking Sexuality*, 20–21.

7. Sam Allberry, "Where to Find Hope and Help amid the Sexual Revolution," The Gospel Coalition, November 5, 2018, https://www.thegospelcoalition .org/article/hope-help-sexual-revolution/. It is also a reminder for us that when God gives us a command, he frequently promises his presence and/or power to help. See Darby Strickland, "When a Command Became a Promise," Christian Counseling & Educational Foundation, November 6, 2019, https:// www.ccef.org/when-a-command-became-a-promise/.

8. All the skills of a discipler come to bear in conversations like this. Before you talk to your teenager, review these skills in our companion book, Deepak Reju and Jonathan D. Holmes, *Rescue Skills: Essential Skills for Restoring the Sexually Broken* (Phillipsburg, NJ: P&R Publishing, 2021).

9. Tim Challies, "Has Your Child Been Looking at Bad Stuff Online?" *Challies* (blog), January 15, 2019, https://www.challies.com/vlog/has-your-child-been -looking-at-bad-stuff-online/.

10. Tim Challies, *Help! My Kids Are Viewing Pornography* (Wapwallopen, PA: Shepherd Press, 2017), 35.

11. See Jay Stringer, *Unwanted: How Sexual Brokenness Reveals Our Way to Healing* (Colorado Springs: NavPress, 2018), 149.

12. Julie Lowe, *Child Proof: Parenting by Faith Not Formula* (Greensboro, NC: New Growth Press, 2018), 80.

13. Matt Fradd, *The Porn Myth: Exposing the Reality behind the Fantasy of Pornography* (San Francisco: Ignatius Press, 2017), 167.
14. Lowe, *Child Proof*, 93. See also Ps. 16:6.
15. Fradd, *Porn Myth*, 163.
16. Luke Gilkerson, "Accountability as a Lifestyle (Part 3): The Next Generation," Covenant Eyes, February 23, 2011, https://www.covenanteyes.com/2011/02/23/accountability-as-a-lifestyle-part-3-the-next-generation/.

Conclusion: Victory, Better Endings, and a Glorious Savior

1. See Hampton Sides, *Ghost Soldiers: The Forgotten Epic Story of World War II's Most Dramatic Mission* (New York: Doubleday, 2001), 294.
2. See Sides, 295.

Appendix: A Godly Vantage Point on Sex

1. Malcolm Muggeridge, *Tread Softly for You Tread on My Jokes* (Glasgow: Collins, 1966), 46.
2. David Powlison, "Making All Things New: Restoring Pure Joy to the Sexually Broken," chap 4. in *Sex and the Supremacy of Christ*, ed. John Piper and Justin Taylor (Wheaton, IL: Crossway, 2005), 70.
3. See Andreas J. Köstenberger with David W. Jones, *God, Marriage, and Family: Rebuilding the Biblical Foundation*, 2nd ed. (Wheaton, IL: Crossway, 2010), 197.

RESOURCES FOR FIGHTING PORNOGRAPHY

FOR MEN

Challies, Tim. *Sexual Detox: A Guide for Guys Who Are Sick of Porn.* Minneapolis: Cruciform Press, 2010.

Chester, Tim. *Closing the Window: Steps to Living Porn Free.* Downers Grove, IL: IVP Books, 2010.

Croft, Brian. *Help! He's Struggling with Pornography.* Wapwallopen, PA: Shepherd Press, 2014.

Freeman, John. *Hide or Seek: When Men Get Real with God about Sex.* Greensboro, NC: New Growth Press, 2014.

Lambert, Heath. *Finally Free: Fighting for Purity with the Power of Grace.* Grand Rapids: Zondervan, 2013.

Reju, Deepak. *Pornography: Fighting for Purity.* Phillipsburg, NJ: P&R Publishing, 2018.

White, David. *Sexual Sanity for Men: Re-creating Your Mind in a Crazy Culture.* Greensboro, NC: New Growth Press, 2012.

FOR WOMEN

Coyle, Rachel. *Help! She's Struggling with Pornography.* Wapwallopen, PA: Shepherd Press, 2017.

Dykas, Ellen, ed. *Sexual Sanity for Women: Healing from Sexual and Relational Brokenness.* Greensboro, NC: New Growth Press, 2012.

Thorne, Helen. *Purity Is Possible: How to Live Free of the Fantasy Trap.* Epsom, UK: Good Book Company, 2014.

Tiede, Vicki. *When Your Husband Is Addicted to Pornography: Healing Your Wounded Heart.* Greensboro, NC: New Growth Press, 2012.

FOR HUSBANDS AND WIVES

Black, R. Nicholas. *What's Wrong with a Little Porn When You're Married?* Greensboro, NC: New Growth Press, 2017.

Solomon, Curtis. *Redeem Your Marriage: Hope for Husbands Who Have Hurt through Pornography.* Greensboro, NC: New Growth Press, 2022.

Solomon, Jenny. *Reclaim Your Marriage: Grace for Wives Who Have Been Hurt by Pornography.* Greensboro, NC: New Growth Press, 2022.

FOR SINGLES

Black, R. Nicholas. *What's Wrong with a Little Porn When You're Single?* Greensboro, NC: New Growth Press, 2012.

FOR ANYONE

Powlison, David. *Coming Clean: Breaking Pornography's Hold on You.* Greensboro, NC: New Growth Press, 2012.

———. *Making All Things New: Restoring Joy to the Sexually Broken.* Wheaton, IL: Crossway, 2017.

———. *Sexual Addiction: Freedom from Compulsive Behavior.* Greensboro, NC: New Growth Press, 2010.

Roberts, Vaughan. *The Porn Problem: Christian Compassion, Convictions and Wisdom for Today's Big Issues.* Epsom, UK: Good Book Company, 2018.

Smith, Winston T. *The Problem with Masturbation.* Greensboro, NC: New Growth Press, 2009.

FOR PARENTS OF CHILDREN AND TEENAGERS

Challies, Tim. *Help! My Kids Are Viewing Pornography*. Wapwallopen, PA: Shepherd Press, 2017.

Gilkerson, Luke. *The Talk: 7 Lessons to Introduce Your Child to Biblical Sexuality*. Self-pub., CreateSpace, 2014.

Gilkerson, Luke, and Trisha Gilkerson. *Changes: 7 Biblical Lessons to Make Sense of Puberty*. Self-pub., CreateSpace, 2015.

Jenson, Kristen. *Good Pictures Bad Pictures: Porn-Proofing Today's Young Kids*. 2nd ed. Kennewick, WA: Glen Cove Press, 2018.

Perritt, John. *Not If, But When: Preparing Our Children for Worldly Images*. Fearn, UK: CF4Kids, 2020.

FOR CHILDREN AND TEENAGERS

Holcomb, Justin S., and Lindsey A. Holcomb. *God Made All of Me: A Book to Help Children Protect Their Bodies*. Greensboro, NC: New Growth Press, 2015.

Jones, Stan, and Brenna Jones. *Facing the Facts: The Truth about Sex and You*. 3rd ed. God's Design for Sex 4. Colorado Springs: NavPress, 2019.

———. *The Story of Me: Babies, Bodies, and a Very Good God*. 3rd ed. God's Design for Sex 1. Colorado Springs: NavPress, 2019.

———. *What's the Big Deal? Why God Cares about Sex*. 3rd ed. God's Design for Sex 3. Carol Stream, IL: NavPress, 2019.

Nystrom, Carolyn. *Before I Was Born: God Knew My Name*. 3rd ed. God's Design for Sex 2. Colorado Springs: NavPress, 2019.

Ryle, J. C. *Thoughts for Young Men*. 1886. Reprint, Amityville, NY: Calvary Press, 1996.

Deepak Reju (MDiv, PhD, The Southern Baptist Theological Seminary) is pastor of the biblical counseling and family ministries at Capitol Hill Baptist Church in Washington, DC. He is the editor of the 31-Day Devotionals for Life series and the author of a number of books, including *Pornography: Fighting for Purity* and *On Guard: Preventing and Responding to Child Abuse at Church*. He serves on the Biblical Counseling Coalition's board of directors and is a trustee for the Christian Counseling & Educational Foundation (CCEF). Deepak is married to Sarah, and they have two sons and three daughters.

Jonathan D. Holmes (MA, Trinity Evangelical Divinity School) is the founder and executive director of Fieldstone Counseling and the pastor of counseling for Parkside Church Bainbridge and Green. He is the author of several books, including *Counsel for Couples: A Biblical and Practical Guide for Marriage Counseling*; a frequent speaker at conferences and retreats; and a trustee for the Christian Counseling & Educational Foundation (CCEF). Jonathan is married to Jennifer, and they have four daughters.

Did you find this book helpful?
Consider leaving a review online.
The authors appreciate your feedback!

Or write to P&R at editorial@prpbooks.com
with your comments. We'd love to hear from you.

THE NEXT STEP IN YOUR FIGHT AGAINST PORN

In *Rescue Skills*, we offer specific skills for your toolbox, so you can be better equipped to engage friends who are struggling with pornography and masturbation.

"Has the potential to . . . change the way you offer ministry to women and men who battle sexual sin."
  —**Ellen Mary Dykas**, Women's Ministry Director, Harvest USA

"The most realistic-yet-hope-filled book I've read on helping people with pornography."
  —**Alasdair Groves**, Executive Director, Christian Counseling & Educational Foundation

"Compassionate, fresh, practical, convicting, and reproducible . . . the right book at the right time."
  —**Dave Harvey**, President, Great Commission Collective

ALSO BY DEEPAK REJU

PORNOGRAPHY

FIGHTING
FOR
PURITY

31-DAY DEVOTIONALS FOR LIFE

DEEPAK REJU

Is there any hope for those in the "voluntary slavery" of pornography addiction? Deepak Reju points out that this worship problem can be fought only with a greater love for Christ. This monthlong devotional, with reflection questions and practical suggestions for action, gives you the daily encouragement and preparation you need for the war being waged for your soul every day.

"Reju's work on pornography is relentlessly biblical, consistently practical, and wonderfully aggressive in laying out the need for godly community and humility. I have worked with many who struggled with pornography, and I wish I had had this resource to give to each of them!"
—**Alasdair Groves**, Executive Director, Christian Counseling & Educational Foundation

In the 31-Day Devotionals for Life series, biblical counselors and Bible teachers guide you through Scripture passages that speak to specific situations or struggles, helping you to apply God's Word to your life in practical ways day after day.

ALSO FROM P&R PUBLISHING ON ADDICTION

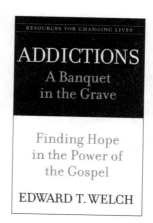

Scripture reveals addicts' true condition: like guests at a banquet thrown by "the woman Folly," they are already in the grave (Prov. 9:13–18). Can we not escape our addictions? Following Jesus, we have "immense hope that God can give power so that we are no longer mastered by the addiction."

"Destroys the myth that addiction is a disease and sin is a sickness. must be replaced with the biblical view of sin, salvation, and sanctification. As a pastor, biblical counselor, and redeemed (not recovering) ex-heroin addict, I believe Welch has given every pastor, parishioner, and anyone caught in the bondage of idolatry/addiction a biblical road map to lasting freedom."
—**Peter Garich**, Dayspring Center for Biblical Counseling

ALSO FROM P&R PUBLISHING
ON FIGHTING SEXUAL SIN

When the heart is filled with rage, sensuality, or pride, sexual fantasy all too easily leads to acts that were previously unimaginable. Biblical counselor John Street takes a hard look at the underlying idolatries that lead even Christians to commit egregious sexual sins. And he shows how Christ gives men and women abundant grace and strength to say no to the fleshly desires and humbly live for him.

"The unfolding of the truth about the heart is for any malady of the soul. This book can instruct the reader to develop good devotional and Bible-reading habits to overcome the temptations of sin in all areas of life. This book contains so many jewels for understanding the heart that reading it [is] like searching for gold."
— **Bill Shannon**, Pastor of Discipleship Counseling, Grace Community Church, Sun Valley, California

"The survey of diagnostic questions is itself worth the price of the book."
— **Stuart W. Scott**, Professor of Biblical Counseling, The Master's University